HISTORY AROUND US 2

Saxon and Norman Britain

Henry Pluckrose

Mills & Boon Limited
London, Toronto, Sydney

First published 1979

text © Henry Pluckrose 1979

ISBN 0 263 06390 9

Maps drawn by Reproduction Drawings Ltd.,
Sutton, Surrey

Filmset and printed in Great Britain by
BAS Printers Limited, Over Wallop, Hampshire
and bound by Hunter & Foulis Ltd., Edinburgh
for the Publishers Mills & Boon Ltd.,
17–19 Foley Street, London W1A 1DR.

contents

1. Setting the Scene 410–1100   9
2. At Home   32
3. At Work   40
4. At Play   45
5. At War   48
6. At Law   57
7. At Prayer   62
   Museums of Special Interest   77

Hadrian's Wall at Housesteads, Northumberland
The building of the wall was commissioned by the Emperor Hadrian in 122 to defend the Roman province of Britain against raids from the barbarian tribes of Picts and Scots. The wall ran from Solway Firth in the West to the estuary of the River Tyne in the East, a distance of 117 km (72 miles). It stood about 4.5 m high and was topped with a parapet. On either side of the wall was a deep ditch.

The wall was manned by 15,000 auxiliary troops who lived in large forts along its length. There were also milecastles (each with a garrison of between 25–30 men) and turrets which served as lookout posts and signal stations.

Hadrian's Wall was finally abandoned in 383 A.D. (Photograph A. F. Kersting)

1 setting the scene
410~1100

It's a striking thought, that we are tomorrow's history. Our buildings, tools, furniture and fabric will be studied by historians of the future who wish to learn something of life in Britain in the 1980s. Archaeologists might even be commissioned to undertake a dig on some long-disused Battle of Britain airfield looking for evidence to substantiate a document or map uncovered in the attic of a late Elizabethan (c. 1978) house.

The fascinating thing about history is that it is about people, people like us. They were born, they grew up, raised a family, aged and died. They built houses, invented tools and fashioned wood and iron to make weapons to defend themselves against their enemies. They knew how to grow food, keep cattle and spin wool to weave cloth. They designed ships to travel upon water and carts to travel across land. They made marks upon stone, wood, clay and parchment telling of their achievements and beliefs.

For convenience, but for no other reason, we tend to lump history into periods. In Britain, for example, the Romans were followed by Saxons, Vikings and Normans, a pattern our history books faithfully

Portchester Castle, Hampshire
The forts of the Saxon shore were probably built to protect Roman Britain from sea raiders (Frisians, Saxons, Angles and Jutes) from across the North Sea. Some historians, however, suggest that the term 'Saxon shore' means that this was an area settled by barbarians from Jutland and Saxony.

The forts stretched along the coast from the Wash to the Isle of Wight. Portchester was built in about 280 A.D. and occupied until 370 A.D. Like most Roman forts the plan was based upon the square, the defensive wall being strengthened along its length with projecting bastions.

In Norman times a stone keep was built in the North West corner of the Roman fort. This photograph also shows the 12th century church of St. Mary. (Photograph Cambridge University collection)

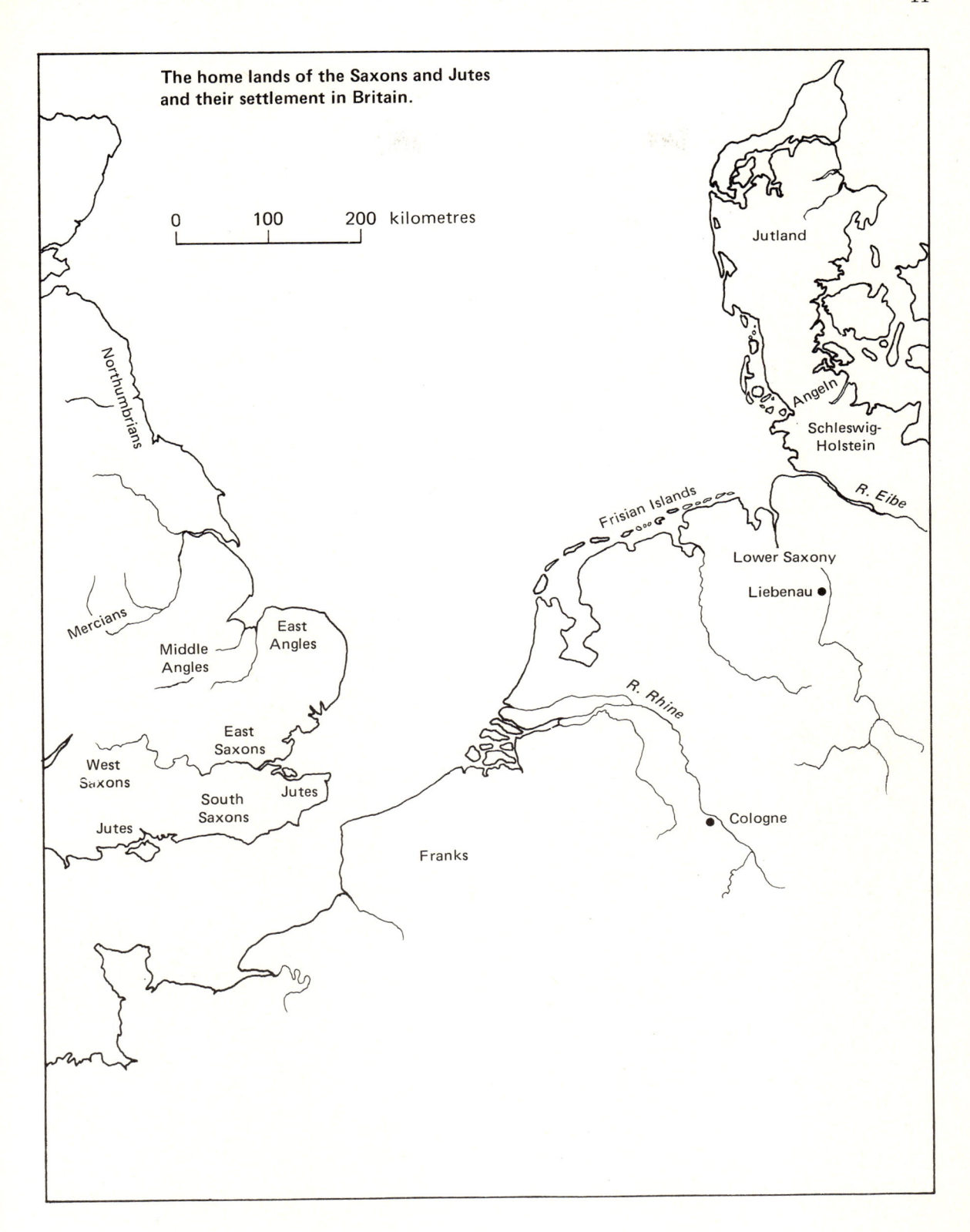

The home lands of the Saxons and Jutes and their settlement in Britain.

reflect. When treating history in this way, however, we tend to forget that the change from one period to the next was a gradual one. Some dates and events might seem (900 years later) to mark a change in direction, a new beginning. I feel certain, however, that the people who were living in Northumberland in 1066 died quite unaware of the fact that they had lived through a momentous year in the history of England. Their life had gone on much as before. There had been talk of a battle in the south, rumours of a new king, a new lord to serve, but the crops still had to be harvested, the children to be fed and the cattle to be killed and salted for the coming winter.

This book, then, is a little different from some you might read. It covers almost 700 years of history, tracing the past through the evidence that we can actually see around us—in the countryside, at historic sites and in museums. It is concerned with the period between the departure of the Romans and the establishment of the Norman kings in England. Before we are able to appreciate the things we can see and the places we can visit, it is important to understand something of the main events of these times.

Saxon Houses at West Stow, Suffolk
At West Stow in Suffolk a Saxon site has been extensively excavated. From the evidence of the foundations of the buildings which were uncovered reconstructions were made of the Saxon hall and the sunken huts. The photograph shows two 'halls' (where the families lived). The sunken hut (sometimes called a Grubenhaus) is on the right. These huts were probably used for sleeping and for storage. The pit over which they were erected varied in depth from 50 cm to 1.5 metres. The walls were lined with planks of oak and some were also floored. Posts supported the thatched roof. A number of the sunken huts excavated at West Stow had hearths. These were placed at the side of the hut and not in the centre.
(Photograph Suffolk Archaeological Unit)

BURHS FOUNDED IN ALFRED'S REIGN

Britain was part of the Roman Empire until the year 410. The last years of the Empire, however, were far from peaceful. In 367 the Barbarians had attacked from the North (the Picts), the East (the Saxons) and the West (the Irish). The invaders were pushed back, but it was clear that the defences of the province were a little weak. The forts of the Saxon shore had failed to contain the Saxon invaders and Hadrian's Wall could only be held against prolonged attack if there were sufficient trained troops to man it.

The Saxons were a Germanic people and, like many of the barbarian tribes, were prepared to fight alongside the Romans. Some of the Saxon mercenary soldiers fought in Britain. On retiring from the army, they settled in the country. An example of this can be seen at West Stowe, near Bury St. Edmunds, where archaeologists have been working on a settlement which seems to have been a village for Saxon people working in the Roman town of Icklingham. The pottery which has been excavated indicates that the settlement dates from before the year 400, some years before the Roman army was finally withdrawn from Britain to defend Rome.

In 410, with the departure of the last legions, the Saxons began to explore the coastline and rivers of Britain with even more determination than before. At first the attacks were little more than pirate raids. The country, however, was comparatively prosperous and settlement became a more attractive prospect than plunder. When the Britons begged the Roman Emperor, Honorious, for help to defend the province, he refused. Facing attacks from both Saxon and Pict, the British leaders tried to do what the Romans had done for so long, so successfully. They decided to employ mercenary soldiers to fight for them. The Anglo Saxon Chronicle tells us what happened. 'Hengist and Horsa were invited by Vortigern, king of the Britons, and they came to Britain at a place called Ebbsfleet (Sandwich, Kent). First they came to help the Britons, but then they fought against them'. Some historians believe that Hengist and Horsa had once served in the Roman army, certainly their coming marked a new phase in the expansion of Saxon dominance.

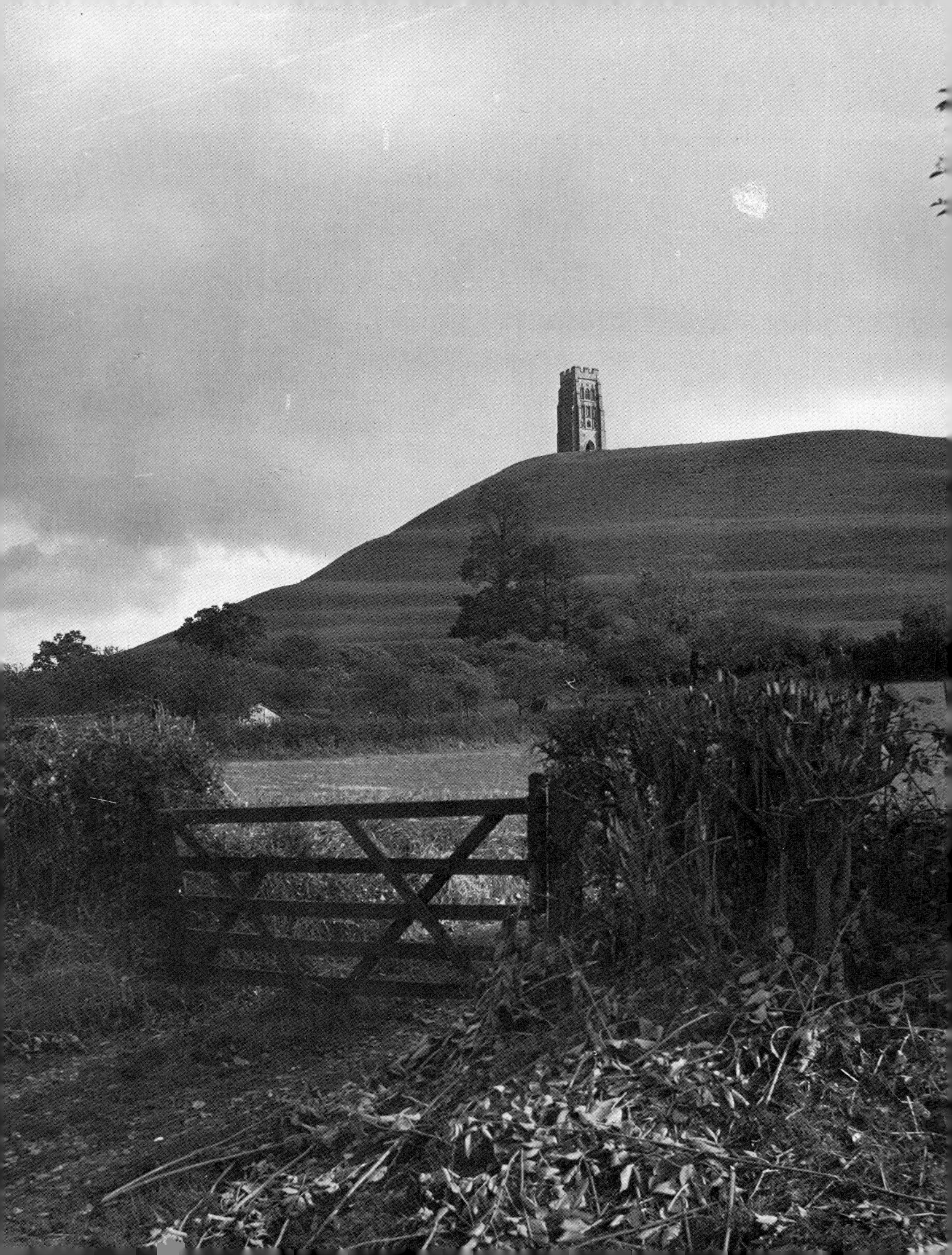

Glastonbury Tor

Glastonbury Tor stands in an area of meadow land which was, until recent times, often flooded. Glastonbury has many legendary links with King Arthur. It was to Glastonbury that Joseph of Arimathaea was said to have brought the Holy Grail, the chalice that Christ used at the last supper. When he reached Glastonbury, the story continues, he stuck his staff into the earth whereupon it changed into a flowering thorn. Arthur and Guinevere are buried in the grounds of Glastonbury Abbey.
(Photograph A. F. Kersting)

Although they were slowly pushed westwards, the Britons did not give up easily. Ambrosius Aurelianus is the most famous Celtic leader of this period. He defeated the Saxons at the Battle of Mount Badon in 490 using cavalry with considerable effect. The stories which were told about him are close to the legend of King Arthur, a warrior leader whose mounted knights fought against the powers of evil. The headquarters of Ambrosius Aurelianus might well have been on Cadbury Hill (the Camelot of the King Arthur legend).

The defiance of leaders like Ambrosius, however, was short lived. Soon the Saxons, settling along rivers and coasts, following old trackways and the Roman roads, formed small kingdoms of their own. Wessex, Sussex, Kent, Essex, Northfolk (Norfolk), Southfolk (Suffolk), Mercia (Midlands), Deira (mainly Yorkshire), Bernicia (north Yorkshire) slowly evolved into five principal kingdoms. These were Northumbria (Britain north of the Humber), Mercia (Midlands between Rivers Thames and Severn), Wessex (Sussex to Devon), Kent and East Anglia.

Tintagel 'King Arthur's Castle' Cornwall
(and overleaf)

Tintagel has links with King Arthur. Here Arthur's parents (King Uther Pendragon and Ygraine) met and fell in love.

A monastery was founded on the site in about 500 by St. Juliot. This remained until 1086 when the monks left. Although some of the foundations of the Celtic Church can still be seen, most of the present ruins date from the castle built in 1145 by Reginald, Earl of Cornwall (son of Henry I).
(Photograph Kenneth Scowen)

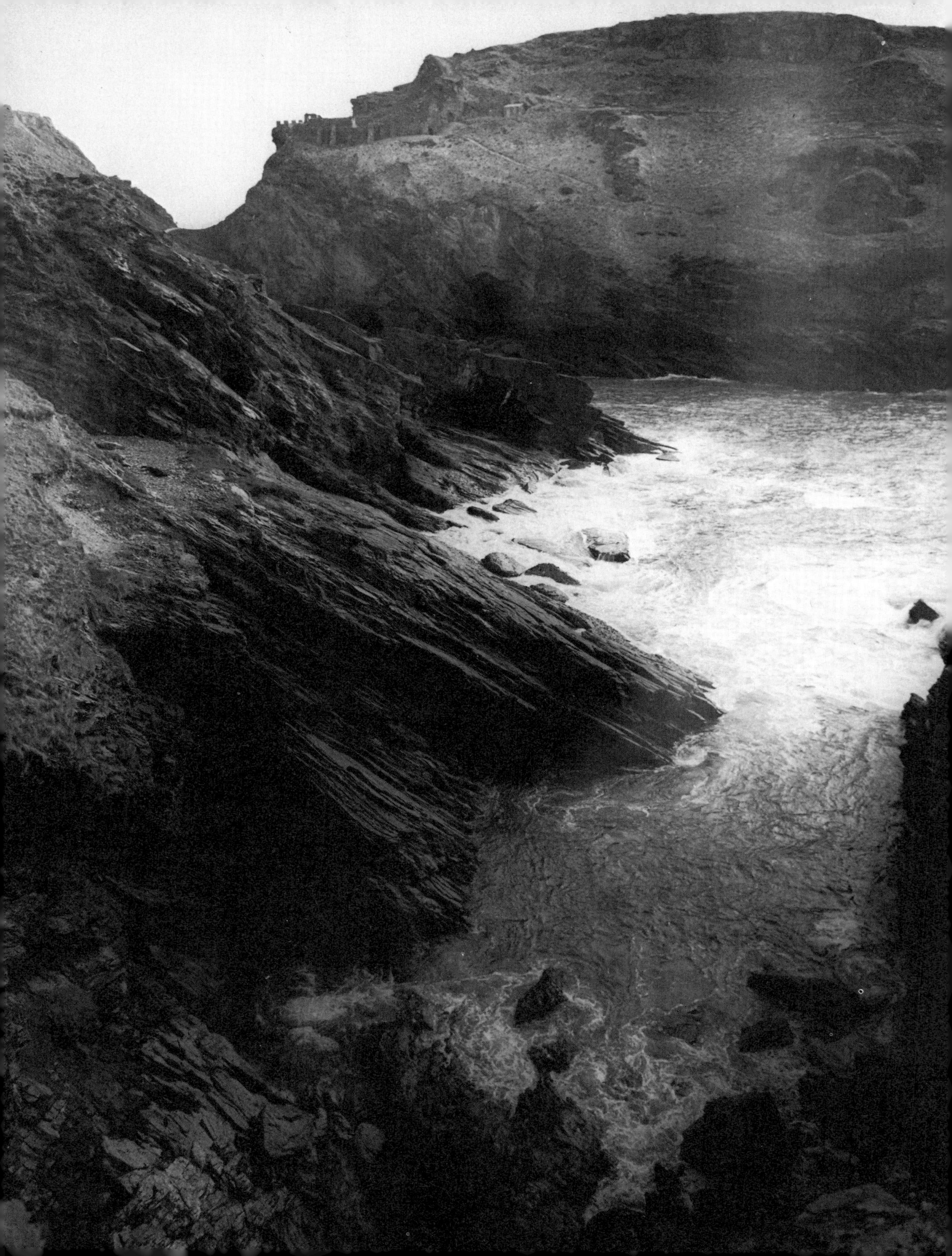

Peddars Way, Norfolk
Peddars Way is an old trackway which runs across Norfolk. It has been in use since pre Roman times and can still be walked today.
(Photograph Edwin Smith)

Clapper Bridge
The Saxon invaders settled along the coast and advanced inland along river valleys. Although rivers provided a means of transport, sometimes they were a barrier. When the water was too deep to wade through, clapper bridges (stepping stones joined by 'flag' stones) were built. This bridge is at East Leach, Gloucestershire.
(Photograph Henry Pluckrose)

The Roman road pattern — which continued to be used in Saxon times

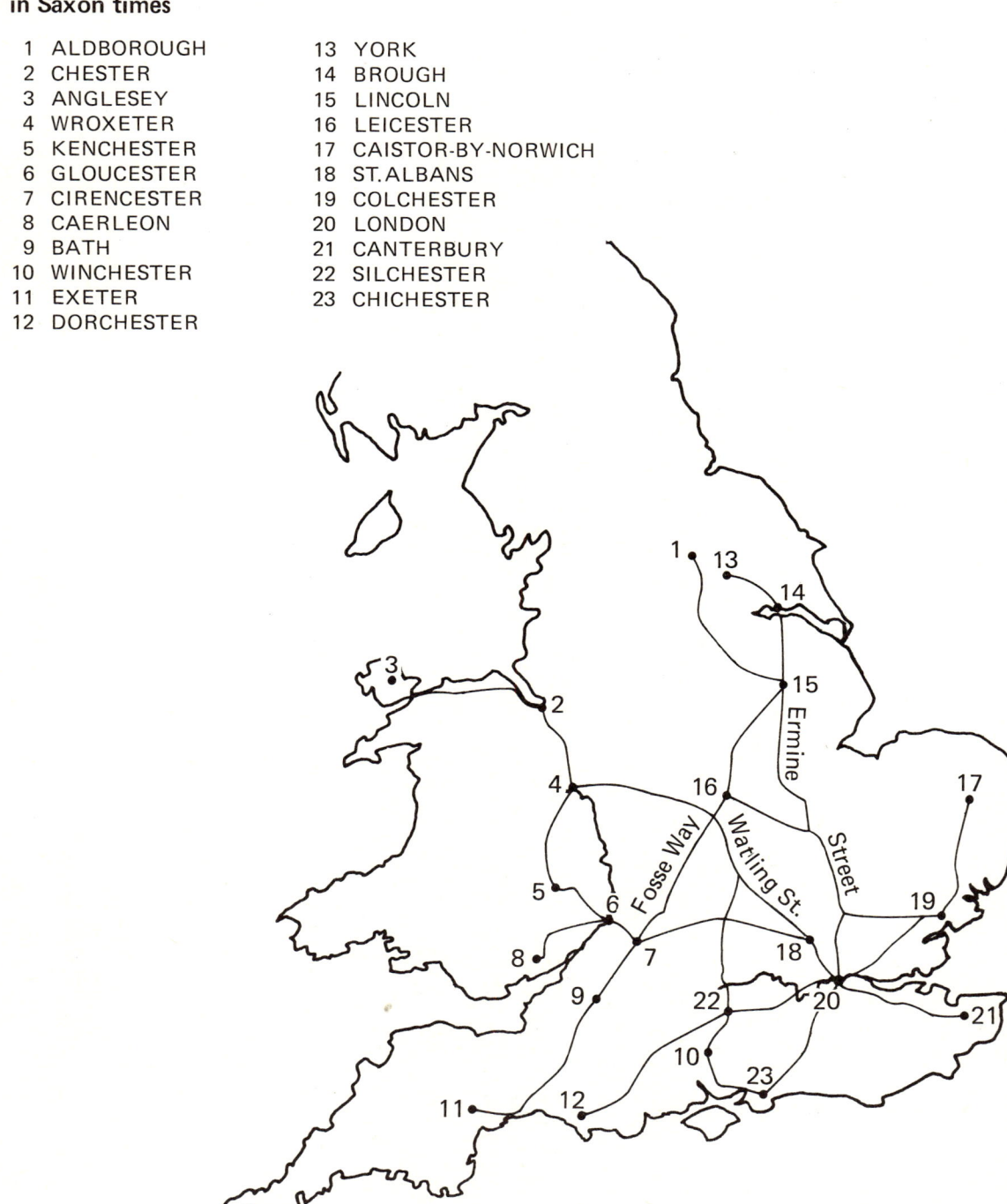

1 ALDBOROUGH
2 CHESTER
3 ANGLESEY
4 WROXETER
5 KENCHESTER
6 GLOUCESTER
7 CIRENCESTER
8 CAERLEON
9 BATH
10 WINCHESTER
11 EXETER
12 DORCHESTER
13 YORK
14 BROUGH
15 LINCOLN
16 LEICESTER
17 CAISTOR-BY-NORWICH
18 ST. ALBANS
19 COLCHESTER
20 LONDON
21 CANTERBURY
22 SILCHESTER
23 CHICHESTER

The emergence of these kingdoms was not without bloodshed. The centre of power moved from one kingdom to another. It was religion rather than kinship which united them.

Christianity had come to Britain in Roman times. With the coming of the Saxons Christianity was kept alive in those areas which remained Celtic: principally, Cornwall, Wales, Scotland, Ireland. The Celtic christians (like Aiden, Columba and Oswold) were missionaries and brought Christianity back to the north of Britain. In the south, christian teaching and religious practice was based upon quite a different source—Rome. In 597 Pope Gregory the Great sent St. Augustine, Prior of the monastery of St. Andrews in Rome, to Britain. He landed in the kingdom of Kent whose Queen, Bertha, was already a Christian. Four years later on Easter Day 601 King Ethelbert and his court were baptized.

Christianity, then, came to the Saxon kingdoms from two sources—the Celtic North (King Edwin of Northumbria was converted in 626) and the 'Roman' South.

As Christianity spread differences in teaching became apparent. The Church of Rome had order, its pattern of worship was clearly defined. The Celtic Church was freer, a little less disciplined. To resolve the differences King Oswy of Northumberland encouraged both parties to meet. They did so at Whitby in the years 663–664. The

Whitby Abbey, Yorkshire *(overleaf)*
The synod which led to the unification of the Celtic and Roman churches was held at Whitby in 663. This abbey was sacked by the Danes in 867. The ruins pictured here belong to the monastery which was refounded in 1067.
(Photograph Henry Pluckrose)

The Chapel of St. Peter, Bradwell, Essex *(Below)*
The church of St. Peter-on-the-Wall, Bradwell, is one of the oldest churches in England. It was built by St. Cedd, Bishop of the East Saxons in 654 and was probably the first cathedral in Essex. Many Roman tiles have been incorporated in the building. These were taken from the Roman fort of Othona which stood on the same site. Othona was one of the Forts of the Saxon shore.

Cedd was trained for the priesthood by Aidan, the Celtic Saint who founded the monastery at Lindisfarne.
(Photograph A. F. Kersting)

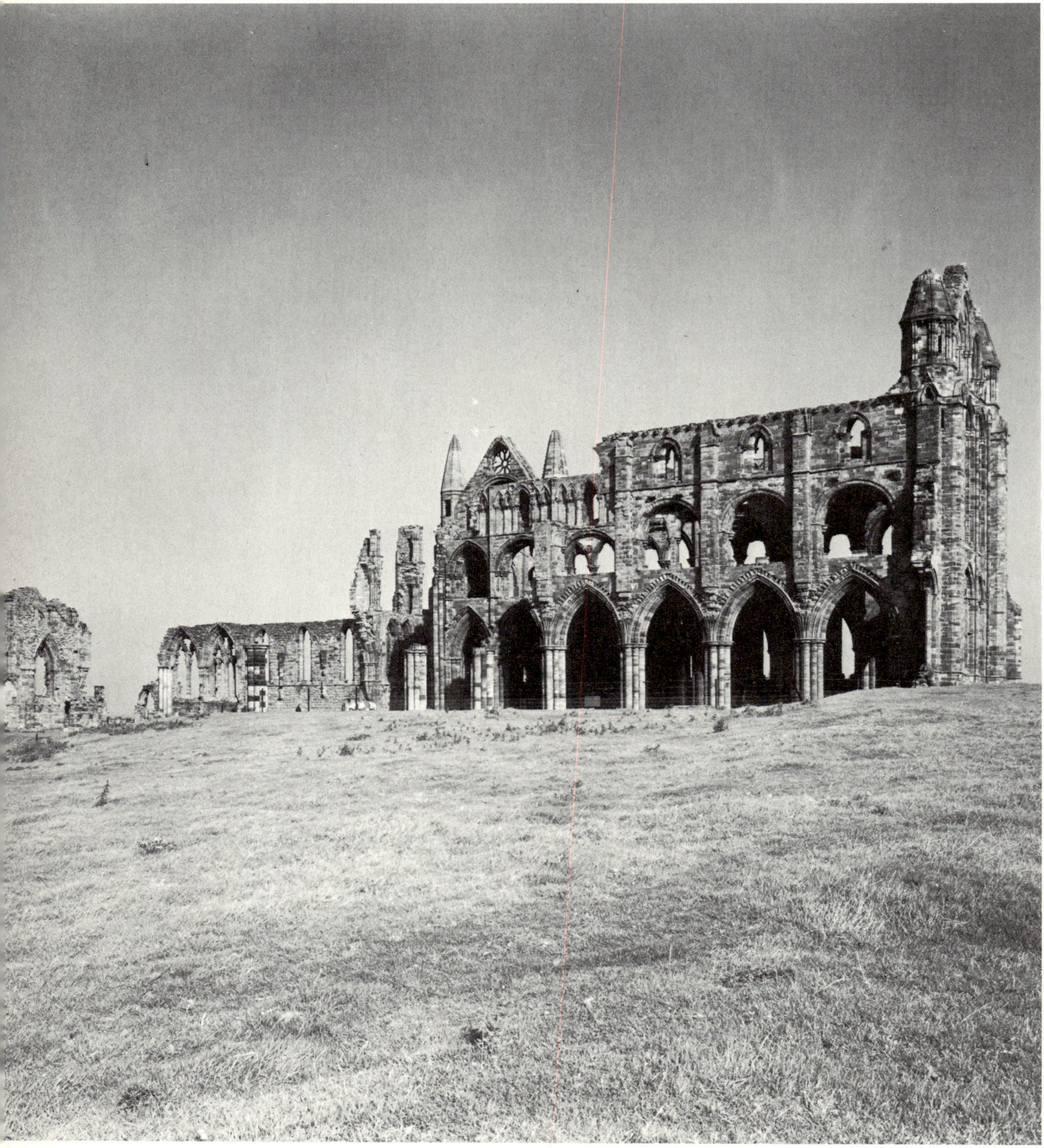

Synod (meeting) confirmed the authority of Rome and the church in Britain was united.

The practice of Christianity led to the building of churches and the founding of cathedrals and monasteries. By the year 790, the Saxon kingdoms were nominally christian, although older heathen customs were still practised. This was not surprising. Gregory had told Augustine that the process of conversion would not be easy. 'Do not pull down heathen temples. Let them become temples of the true God so that people will not have to change their place of worship.' Thus many an early Christian church was built upon the site of a heathen temple. Numerous examples of this dual belief (of the need to observe both a Christian and a Heathen God) can be found. Often they are most clearly indentifiable at death (in grave remains and on memorial stones), but evidence also occurs on the decoration of weapons and ornaments.

North Elmham Cathedral, Norfolk
Elmham was the seat of the Bishop of East Anglia from about 800. In 1075 the church in Thetford was made the centre of the diocese. Soon after this, however, the bishop's seat (or 'Cathedra') was moved to Norwich (where it has remained ever since). The Saxon church was converted into a manor house by the Bishop of Norwich in 1386.
(Photograph Dept. of Environment)

The English kingdoms *c* 700

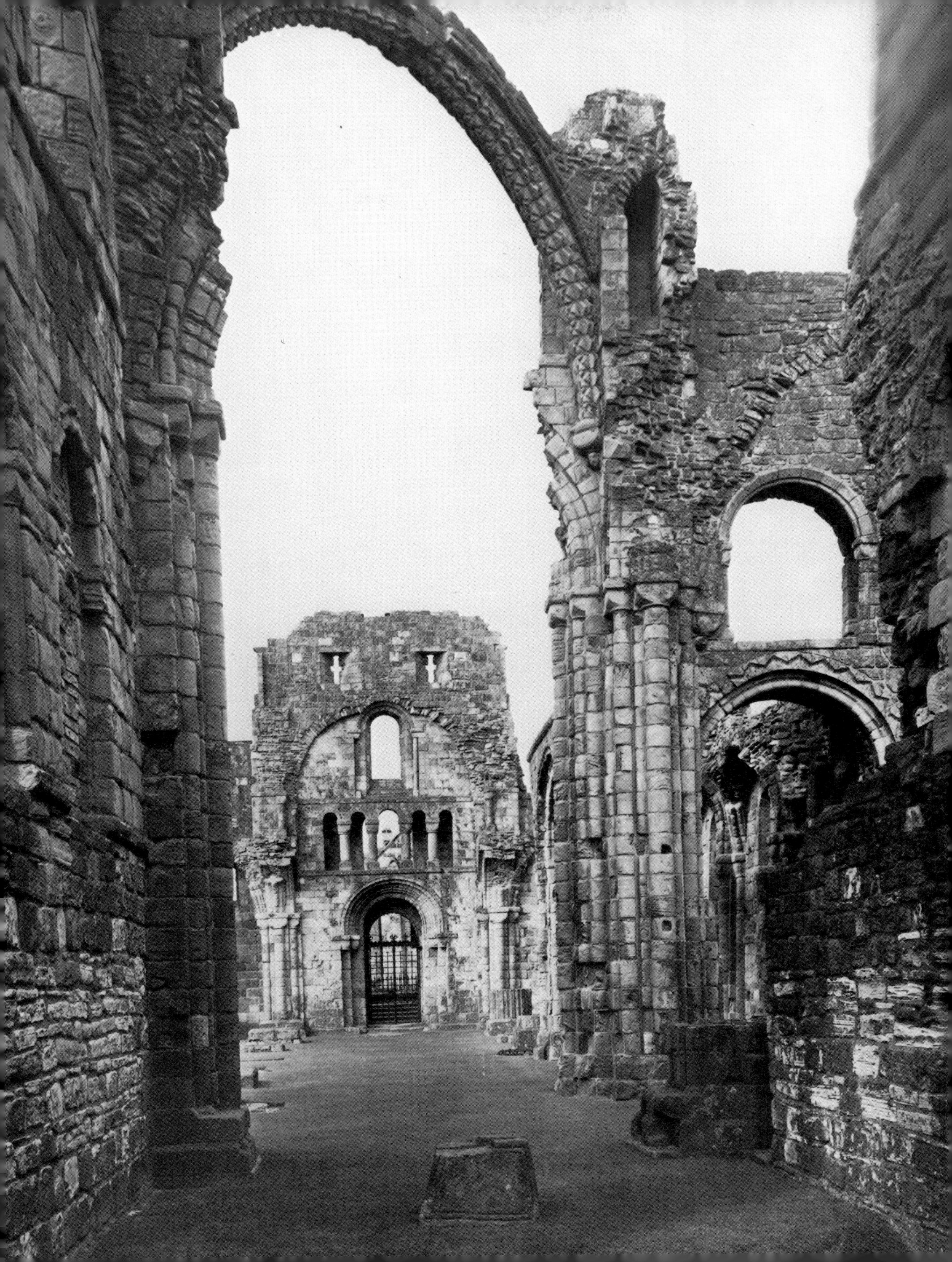

Lindisfarne, Holy Island, Northumberland
(previous page)
Aidan entered the priesthood at Iona, the monastery founded by St. Columba. In 635 his missionary journeys brought him to Lindisfarne where he built a church which was to become an important centre of Christianity. It was this Saxon monastery which was sacked by the Danes in June 793.

The monastery ruins shown here are those of the Benedictine monastery built by the monks of Durham in the 11th century.
(Photograph Dept. of Environment)

The end of the eighth century saw the beginning of a new movement across Europe. Hungry for land upon which to expand, the Vikings or Northmen left Norway, Sweden and Denmark by sea and by land. In 786 three Viking ships landed near Portland Bill and killed the king's reeve, Beaduheard, who had ridden out to enquire their business. This raid set the scene for what was to follow. On 8 June 793 a Viking force attacked Lindisfarne, the monastery of St. Aiden, killing the cattle, looting the church of its treasures, murdering the elderly monks and taking the younger ones away to slavery. 'Lo it is nearly 350 years' (wrote Alcuin, a monk educated in York) 'that we and our fathers have inhabited this lovely land and never before has such terror appeared in Britain as we have now suffered from a pagan race....'

In the following years the Vikings (usually called Danes) returned in search of more plunder. At first the raids only occurred during the summer months. In 851, however, the Danish army wintered on the Isle of Thanet. This was to mark the beginning of Danish settlement, for in 865 the 'great army' arrived, an army which was never to be entirely dislodged from Britain.

It was left to the Anglo Saxon kingdom of Wessex to provide the leadership necessary to halt the Danish expansion. After a series of battles, Alfred's army defeated the Danes at the Battle of Edington (near Westbury in Wiltshire). The peace treaty which followed divided the country into two parts, Wessex and Danelaw (East Anglia, Northumbria, Mercia) and required the Danes to become Christian. Alfred's success, however, was to have a more profound effect. The fact that there was no more land available for them in Britain forced the Danes to look elsewhere. They established kingdoms on the Continent, one of these being Normandy.

Statue of St. Aiden, Lindisfarne, Northumberland
In 635 King Oswold of Northumbria asked the Abbot of Iona for help in bringing Christianity to his kingdom. Aiden, a monk at Iona, was chosen to convert the Northumbrians. He founded the monastery at Lindisfarne and became its abbot. He was also made a bishop—which is why this statue shows him wearing the robes of a monk and holding a crozier, the insignia of a bishop. Aiden died in 651.

The Alfred Jewel
This jewel was found on the Isle of Athelney in Somerset. Around its edge in Anglo-Saxon runs the inscription 'Alfred caused me to be made'.
(Photograph Picturepoint Ltd)

Saxon kingdoms and the first Viking raids

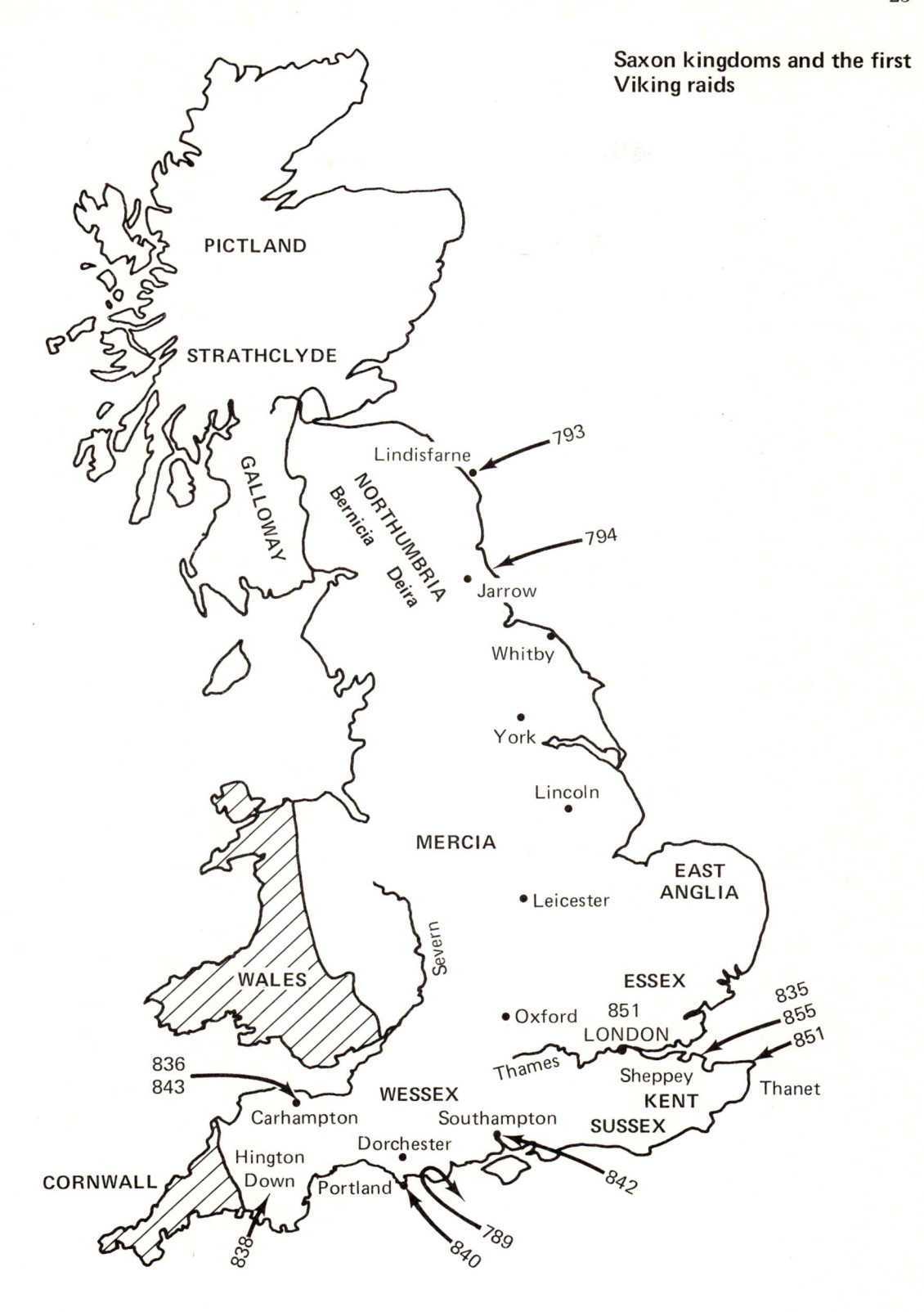

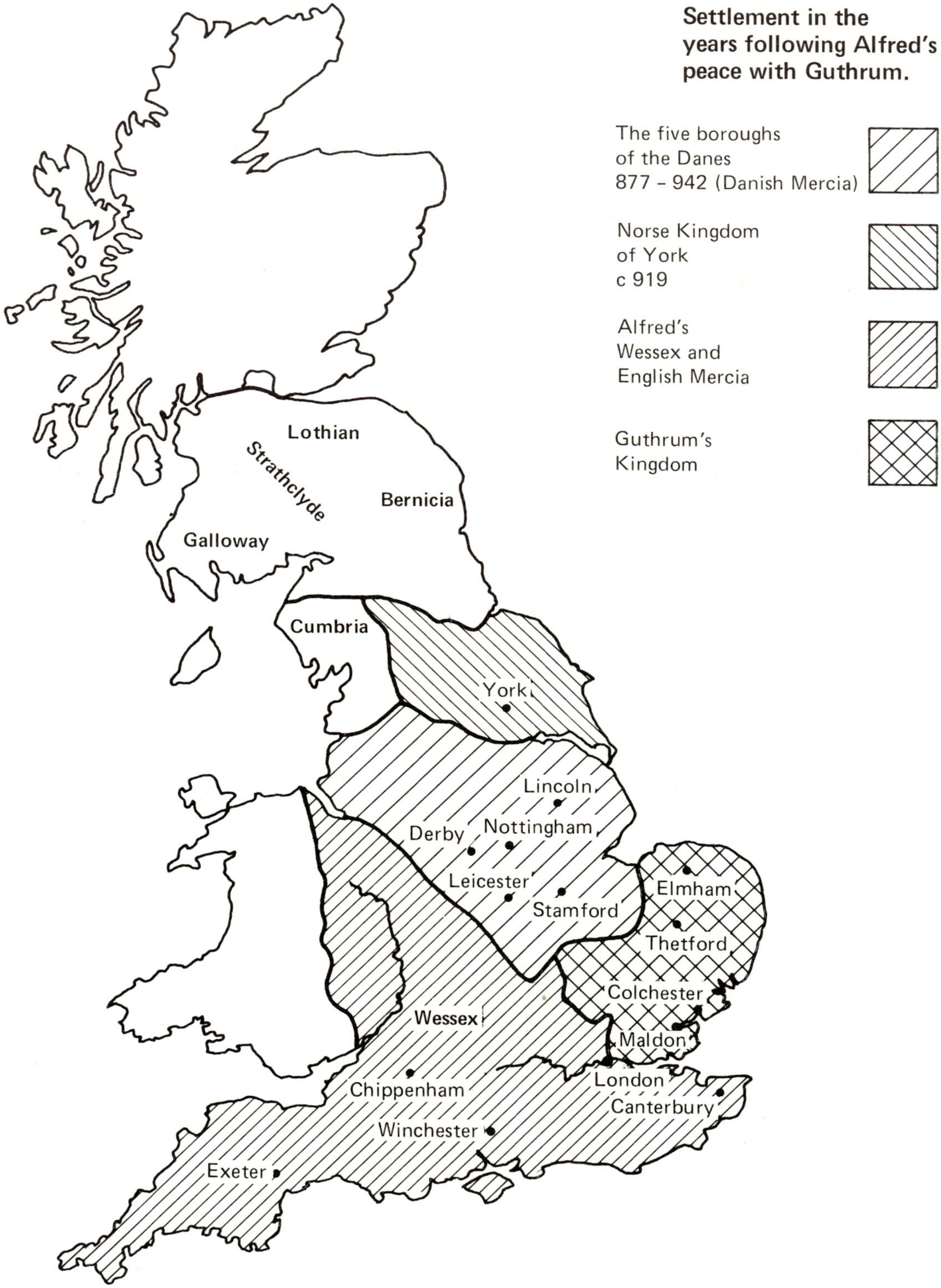
Settlement in the years following Alfred's peace with Guthrum.
The five boroughs of the Danes 877 - 942 (Danish Mercia)
Norse Kingdom of York c 919
Alfred's Wessex and English Mercia
Guthrum's Kingdom
Lothian
Strathclyde
Bernicia
Galloway
Cumbria
York
Lincoln
Derby
Nottingham
Leicester
Stamford
Elmham
Thetford
Colchester
Maldon
Wessex
London
Chippenham
Canterbury
Winchester
Exeter

The Danes who settled in Britain seem to have done so quite quickly. The excavations at York (which was a Danish city) indicate a people skilled in crafts who traded with many parts of Europe and the Middle East. By the time Althelstan, King of Wessex, had reconquered Danelaw (in 924), the Danes were the accepted settlers. Final assimilation of the Danes into Anglo-Saxon society was marked by Edgar the Peaceable (959–75), King of the English, who on his coronation received the submission of the kings of Scotland and the Princes of Wales and 'recognized the customs of the Danes'.

Edgar's son, Ethelred the 'Ill-Advised' (wrongly called 'Unready'), was unable to maintain control over the newly united kingdom. Once more the Danes began to threaten. Ethelred is perhaps best remembered for his attempt to buy off his enemies—to pay money to the Danes to encourage them to withdraw their armies and go elsewhere. The vast quantities of 'danegeld' paid during this period is confirmed by the number and value of Anglo-Saxon coins which have been found in Sweden, Norway and Denmark. Today there is more Anglo Saxon coinage on display in Scandinavian museums than in all the museums in the British Isles!

Ethelred's reign was an unhappy one. He was defeated by Sweyn Forkbeard whose son, Canute, became king. This took England into the Viking Empire of Scandinavia.

The old Anglo Saxon ruling house was, however, soon to return. On the death of Canute, Edward (eventually to be known as the Confessor), the son of Ethelred, succeeded to the throne. Edward was born in Islip in Gloucestershire in about 1002. He spent his early years with the monks in Ely. In 1013 he went to Normandy where he lived until he became king. This was not surprising for his mother, Emma, was a Norman. In Normandy Edward learned Norman ways and customs, many of which he introduced to England during his reign.

Waltham Abbey, Essex
Harold Godwinson built this church in the Norman style in 1060. He did so, according to legend, in thanksgiving for being cured of paralysis after praying at the shrine of The Holy Cross. This relic, a wooden crucifix, had been brought to Essex by Toui, King Canute's standard bearer, who had found it on his land in Somerset. Toui brought it to Waltham and built a small church in which to display it. On being cured, Harold decided the crucifix needed a better home and so he built the abbey.
(Photograph Henry Pluckrose)

Effigy of Robert, Duke of Normandy, Gloucester Cathedral (overleaf)
Robert, known as Curt-hose, was the eldest son of William the Conqueror, who he succeeded as Duke of Normandy. He had a quarrelsome personality and argued with his father and his brothers, William and Henry. After the Battle of Tinchebrai in 1106 Robert was taken prisoner and thrown into prison, where he remained until his death in 1134. His effigy, in Gloucester Cathedral, is of particular interest because it clearly shows the dress and weapons of a Norman knight.   (Photograph A. F. Kersting)

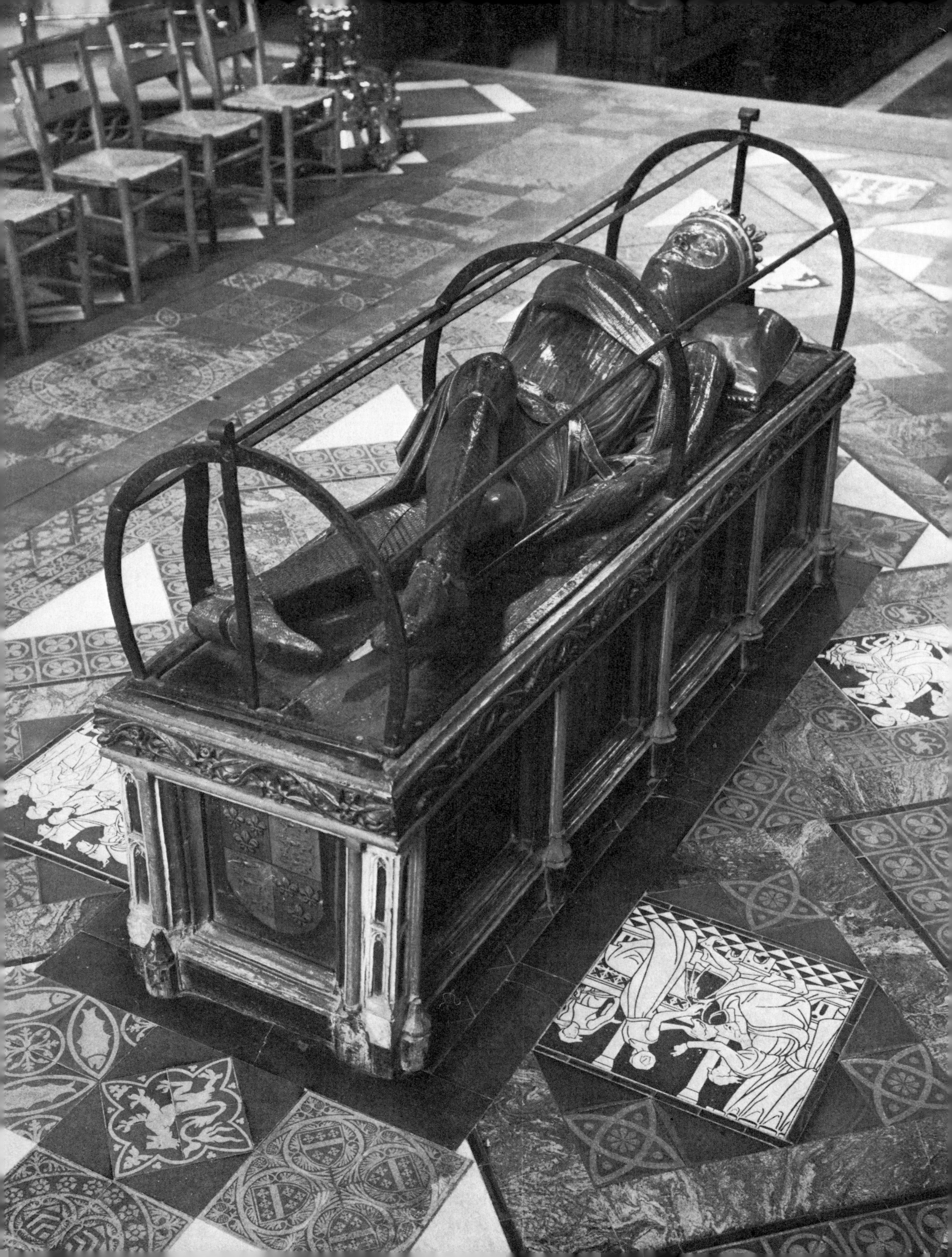

Thus the introduction of Norman ideas did not begin with William I. Harold Godwinson built a great Abbey in the Norman style at Waltham in Essex several years before Edward saw the consecration of his Abbey at Westminster. Similarly, on the borders of Wales, Richard, a Norman knight was given permission to erect a castle, the first to be built in this country. Of this only a few shallow mounds and ditches covered with overgrowth remain. But evidence of Norman influence still exists in the name of the village which grew up around the stronghold, Richard's Castle.

The death of Edward, eight days after the consecration of Westminster Abbey, left the throne of England vacant. There were three strong contenders: Harald Hardrada, King of Norway, William, Duke of Normandy and Harold Godwinson the most powerful earl in England. When the Witan (the Council of Wise Men) chose Harold Godwinson, both William and Harald Hardrada decided to invade and gain the crown by force. The invading armies landed almost simultaneously. In September 1066 King Harold decisively defeated Harald Hardrada and his Norwegian army at the Battle of Stamford Bridge (North Yorkshire). Quickly returning south, Harold's army faced the Norman invaders. On 14 October the two armies met at Hastings in a battle which changed the direction of English history. The Anglo Saxon army was defeated and Harold, together with many of the old nobility, was killed. England was to be tied to Normandy rather than to Scandinavia and England's involvement with France (and with the wars which occupied her kings throughout the Middle Ages) was begun.

It would be wrong, however, to regard William as an alien king. He was a Norman descended from Viking stock claiming sovereignty over an Anglo-Viking people.

The Tomb of Harold, Waltham Abbey, Essex
After the battle of Hastings, Harold's body was identified by Edith Swanneck by 'a special mark only she knew'. His body was brought back to Waltham and buried with his two brothers (who also fell in the battle) near the altar of the church he had founded. (Photograph Henry Pluckrose)

The Norman conquest of England — showing advance to north and west during the years 1066 – 1070

As we have seen there had been strong Norman influence in Edward's day and William certainly saw himself as one who would uphold the old customs and practices of the people. Of course, there were changes, but changes which were probably not immediately apparent to ordinary people. The Normans were invaders bringing with them new ideas of government and kingship. Church (the Pope had blessed William's invasion) and State were united. Bishop and Baron had a common aim, to control their newly won lands and to put down opposition to their rule. The castle and the mounted knight were an effective means of achieving this end.

William, who died in Normandy in 1087, was succeeded by his son William (known as Rufus because of his red hair). William Rufus was not a popular king. The Chronicles describe him as cruel and godless and the latter part of his reign was marked by poor harvests and bad weather.

William's death is surrounded in mystery. He was known to be a superstitious man. Yet, although he had been sleeping badly and troubled with nightmares warning him not to go into the forest, he was determined to hunt. On 2 August 1100, he led a small party of huntsmen into the New Forest. One of his companions was William Tirel or Tyrell. In the late afternoon Tirel and the king surprised a deer. There was a shot and the king fell dying. His body was carried to Winchester by peasants. William of Malmsbury reported that blood dripped from his corpse the whole way. He was buried in the cathedral beneath the tower. The following year the tower collapsed.

Some historians suggest that this was the ritual murder of a king who was beginning to grow old and whose blood had to be shed to give fertility back to the land and so to his people. However, most reject this theory of black magic and attribute the king's murder to a conspiracy to enable his younger brother, Henry, to take the crown.

There is strong support for this, for Henry quickly seized the royal treasure at Winchester. Three days after his brother's death he had himself crowned at Westminster Abbey.

With the death of a king the period covered by this book ends, a period in which the Christian church gives unity to a people; yet behind its flowering there remain shadows of a fiercely pagan past.

The Rufus Stone, New Forest, Hampshire
William II (called Rufus) was killed while hunting in the New Forest. A stone, recording his death, marks the spot. It reads 'Here stood the oak tree at which an arrow shot by Sir Walter Tyrell at a stag glanced and struck King William the Second, surnamed Rufus, on the breast of which he instantly died on the second day of August Anno 1100. King William the Second surnamed Rufus being slain as before related was laid in a cart belonging to one Purkis and drawn from hence to Winchester and buried in the Cathedral Church of that city'.
(Photograph Peter Baker)

2 at home

The Church of St. Andrew, Greensted Juxta Ongar, Essex

The first church at Greensted dates from 600–700 A.D. It, too, was built from logs (staves). Unlike the church which eventually replaced it, the wooden logs were laid directly into the ground. Eventually they rotted. The logs of the present church (which was begun in 845 A.D.) rest on a cill below and fit into a wall plate above. The walls shown here rest upon a brick course, which was added in the 19th century to replace areas of timber which had rotted at ground level.
(Photograph A. F. Kersting)

The Saxons did not settle in the towns which were abandoned by the Britons when the Romans withdrew. Instead they tended to move along river valleys making clearings in the thick forests to grow crops and building houses from the timber. Because wooden buildings do not last for long as buildings made of stone, we have to piece together archaeological evidence if we wish to learn anything of life in a Saxon home. Sufficient material was excavated at West Stowe for houses to be reconstructed using techniques identical to those of the Saxons.

A number of huts (about 4.5 m × 4 m) were grouped around a central hall. Each hut had a planked floor, laid over a shallow pit. This pit might have been used for storage or, alternatively, it served as a damp course to help keep the interior warm and dry. The framework of the house was lashed together without using nails. The spaces between the main beams were filled with a woven framework of hazel and the roof was thatched with straw. These 'houses' might have been used as sleeping quarters or as workshops and storehouses. The families who made up the settlement lived in the Hall, or long house, which served as a living room for the whole community.

The Saxon hall (of which a number have been excavated on the continent) was a long narrow building about four and a half metres wide by ten metres in length. Wooden posts, sunk in individual holes a metre apart, provided the main framework. The walls may have been of wattle or infilled with timber like the walls of the Saxon church of St. Andrew at Greensted-juxta-Ongar in Essex. There were two doors opposite each other in the centre of the longest sides. A hole in the roof served as a chimney.

The Sutton Hoo treasure (now in the British Museum) gives us some idea of the household utensils which would have been found in the home of a rich Saxon. Buckets and tubs made of wood and bonded with

Cauldron and Chain (reconstruction, Sutton Hoo)
This reconstruction, to be seen in the British Museum indicates how skilled the Anglo Saxons were when working in iron. The chain is 3.75 m (12 ft 6 in) long and the cauldron would probably have contained sufficient stew to feed all the oarsmen on a boat at one 'cooking'.
(Photograph Henry Pluckrose)

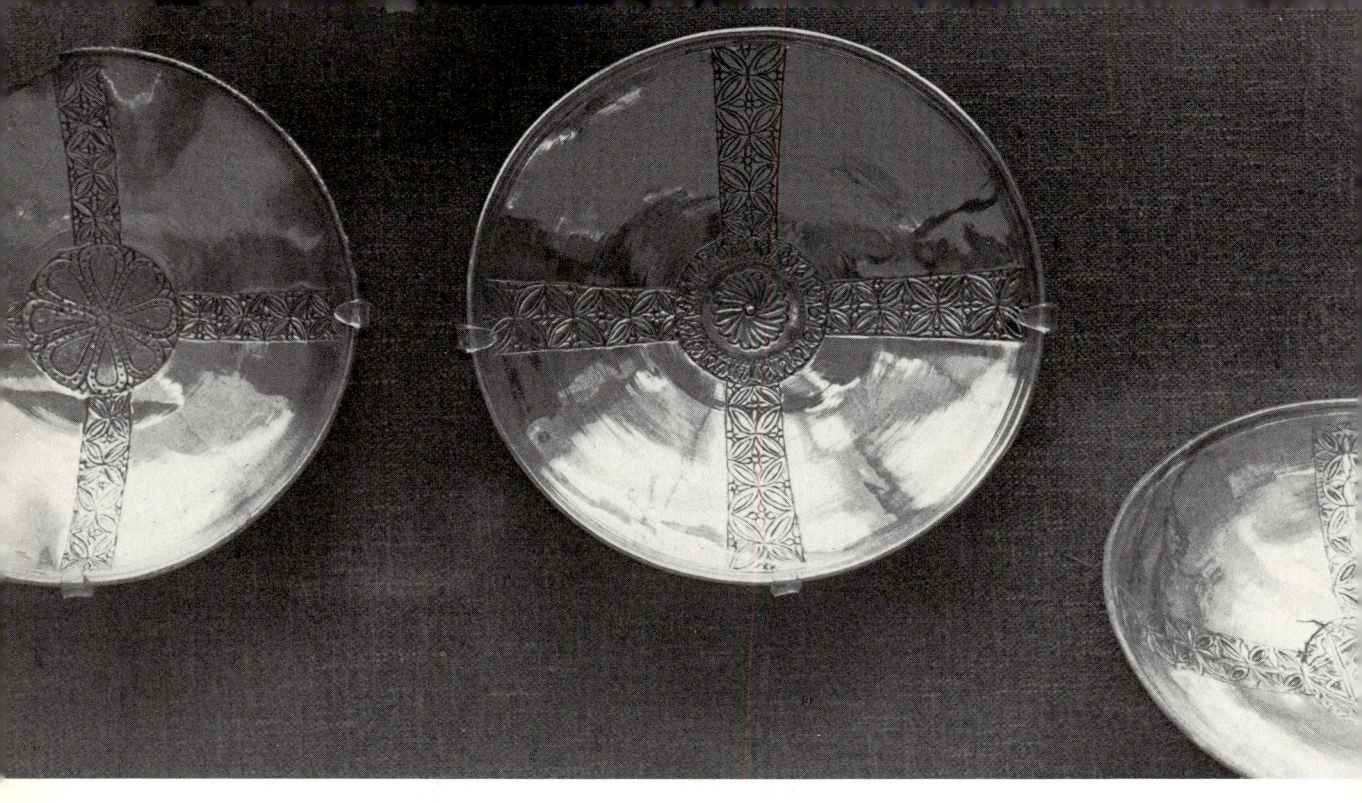

Shallow silver bowl
Seven bowls similar to this were found at Sutton Hoo. Like the spoons they are decorated with Christian rather than pagan symbols. Archaeologists know that bowls identical to this were made in the Eastern Mediterranean—which indicates how far merchants must have travelled in Saxon times.
(Photograph Henry Pluckrose)

Anglo-Saxon Spoons
These silver spoons form part of the Sutton Hoo treasure and are inscribed with the names Saulos and Paulos (Saul and Paul) which suggests that they were a gift to a convert to Christianity (probably King Raedwald who died in about 624/5 A.D.)
(Photograph Henry Pluckrose)

iron, a tripod for holding a cooking pot, dishes of bronze and iron, spoons of silver. He would have drunk spirits from burnwood cups made from walnut and trimmed with silver and ale and mead from horns decorated in silver gilt.

This tells us a great deal about the life style of the rich thane. It is not difficult for us to imagine him dressed in a tunic, his mantle (or cloak) held in position with brooches made of gold and silver, inlaid filigree or 'chip carved' in relief.

The furnishings of his hall, like the hall itself, were made of wood and have long since rotted away. However, illustrations from old manuscripts and written accounts (like Bede's *Ecclesiastical History* and the *Anglo-Saxon Chronicle*) provide much background detail.

Drinking Horns (Sutton Hoo)
These horns and at top of the next page were used for drinking ale or mead (a sweet liquor made from honey). They have silver gilt mounts (open end) and terminate with the delicate head of a bird.
(Photograph Henry Pluckrose)

Spirit Cup
This Burnwood cup, found at Sutton Hoo, was made from walnut trimmed with silver.
(Photograph Henry Pluckrose)

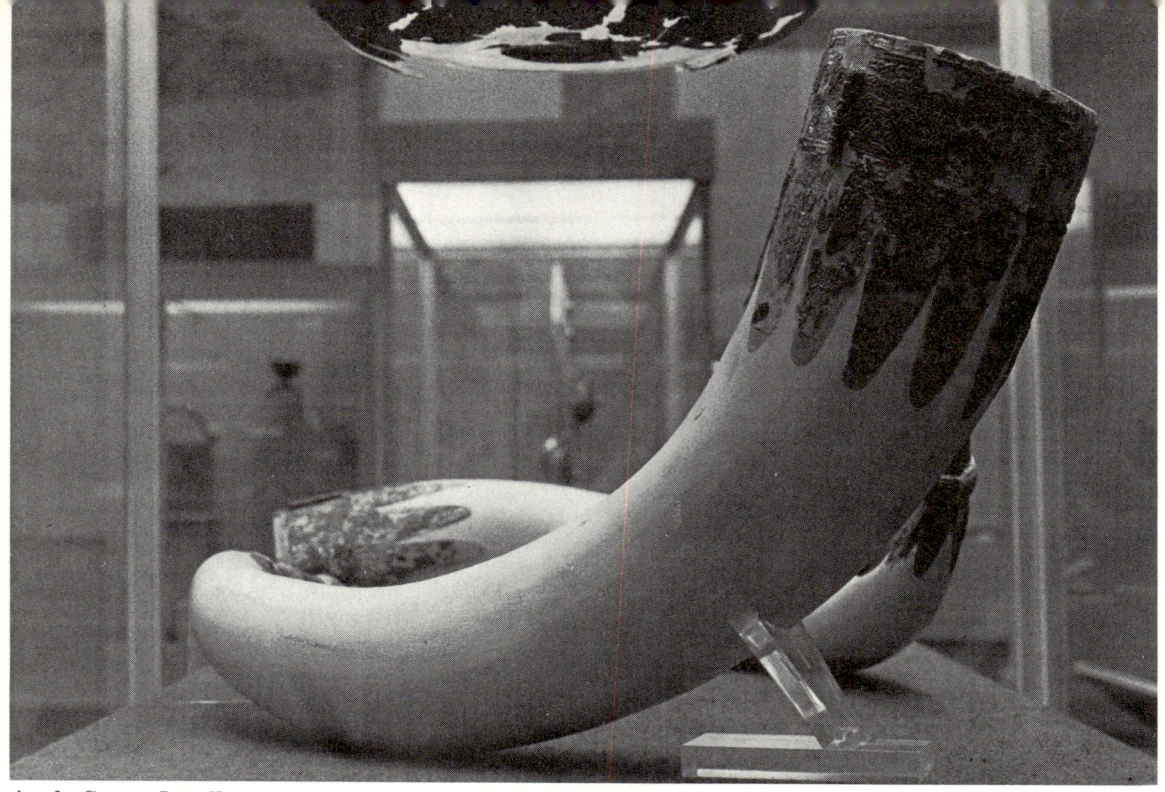

Anglo-Saxon Jewellery
The Anglo Saxons were capable of exquisite work in gold, silver and filigree. These examples may be seen in the British Museum, London. (Photograph British Museum)

Like the Saxons, the Vikings used wood extensively. Excavations of Viking dwellings suggest that they were similar to those of the Saxons. Wooden posts were sunk vertically into the ground, and these supported a roof of thatch or wood. The walls were made of interwoven rods and brushwood coated with mud. In the centre of the hall was the hearth. This was a shallow pit edged with stone to keep the burning logs together. Above it, in the roof, was a hole to allow the smoke to escape. Over the hearth kettles and cauldrons hung on chains. Beside this was the flat stone slab which was used to bake flat cakes of bread which were an important part of the family diet. Around the edge of the hall, and possibly built into its walls, were benches for sitting and sleeping.

Most of the utensils in the hall would also have been made of wood—buckets, plates, bowls and cups. These were strengthened with gilt, bronze and copper.

Excavation of Viking Site, York (1978)
This photograph, taken in August 1978, shows the building methods used by the Vikings at the end of the 10th century. Between the stout wooden posts are walls made by interweaving branches and brushwood. (Photograph Henry Pluckrose)

Tripods, grillspits and cooking pots were made of iron. Personal belongings were kept in chests of oak which also served as chairs and tables. These chests were also taken on board the long boats where they were used as seats for the oarsmen as well as providing dry storage for weapons and equipment.

If the long halls that the Danes built in England were at all similar to those excavated in Scandinavia (and it seems likely that they would have brought traditional methods of building to their new country) then the ends of the hall would have been divided from the main living quarters by wooden screens. One of these smaller rooms often contained an oven; the other was used as a barn or cattle shed.

On large settlements, where a number of families were living in a community, the pathways between the principal halls and store houses were paved with wood. These 'roadways' were made from the trunks of small trees. After trimming, the trunks were laid close together and pegged firmly into the ground.

Meals were taken in the hall. They were served on wooden platters and eaten with knives, spoons and fingers. Forks were unknown. From deposits found in the Viking city of York we know that fish formed an important part of the diet. Bones of both sea fish (cod, haddock, ling, herring, mackerel, scad, thornback ray, conger eel, smelt, flounder and salmon) and fish living in fresh water (pike, perch, roach, chub, dace) have been found.

From stone carvings and the excavation of graves it has been possible to build a very clear idea of Viking dress. The men wore narrow trousers and a wide, hip length, tunic. The cloak was fastened over the right shoulder leaving the sword arm free. It was held in place with a semi-circular brooch or with a ring pin. Viking women wore a long chemise, probably woollen, under a simple full length dress.

On top of this was an over dress consisting of rectangular pieces of cloth front and back which were fastened to each other on the shoulders by a pair of oval 'tortoise' brooches. In the later Viking period these brooches were made larger, probably because they had also to hold a shawl. Both men and women wore shoes of soft leather.

The insignia of the Viking lady was her chatelaine, a metal belt to which were fixed keys and small useful household objects such as scissors, tweezers, needles and combs. She played an important part in the day to day running of the family, being responsible for the defence of the home when her menfolk were away, as well as for all those tasks we associate with home making—having children, preparing food and making clothes from the cloth she had woven from the wool and flax she had spun.

Not all Viking families lived in wooden houses. Some stone farm houses have been discovered, but these are mainly in areas where wood has never been plentiful.

In Norman times stone began to be used rather more extensively for building. The peasant, however, continued to live in a simple timber framed hut with a thatched roof. The richer land holder lived a little more luxuriously but stone houses, even when they were built, were often constructed with defence in mind rather than comfort. An idea of the style of dress and the furnishings of the Norman period can be obtained by studying the Bayeux Tapestry which tells the story of William's successful campaign to gain the English crown.

Carving on 'Warrior Cross', Middleton Church, Nr. Pickering, Yorkshire
This carving shows a Viking surrounded by his weapons—a sword, circular shield, spear and axe. Notice the cap he is wearing and the knife at his waist. The reverse face is filled with a carving of a very twisted dragon.
(Photograph Henry Pluckrose)

Saxon wall and window, Middleton Church, Nr. Pickering, Yorkshire
Saxons and Vikings could build in stone. A number of Saxon churches still exist—as well as the remains of Viking farm houses. Although the wall shown here appears very rough and irregular, great care was taken to strengthen the walls at the corners by using specially selected stones.
(Photograph Henry Pluckrose)

3 at work

Open field strips, Byfield Hill, Nr. Woodford Halse, Northants

Photography from the air has given historians and archaeologists a new dimension to their research. This photograph, taken when the sun was low so that patterns in the land were emphasized by shadow, clearly shows strip cultivation of the fields. (Aerofilms Ltd.)

Apart from the king, the most important member of Saxon society was the thane. The thane lived on an estate (called a vill) and in exchange for the king's protection promised to fight for the king when necessary, to defend his vill against attack and to see that the bridges on his estate were kept in good repair. In turn, the thane gave protection to those who lived on the vill. Below the thane came the cottar (peasant) who was expected to pay for this protection by working on the thane's land for one day a week and for three days in harvest time. Apart from this he was left free to grow his own crops on the five acres of land that was allotted to him. The villein (or gebur) was tied more closely to the thane. He was allowed to work up to 30 acres, but in exchange for this (and the thane's protection) he worked for between two and three days each week on the thane's land. Inferior in status to both cottar and gebur was the slave.

We can trace some of these Anglo Saxon estates by studying the names of our villages and towns. For example, feld (Enfield, Hatfield) meant an open space; mersc (Mere, Marton) a marsh; tun an enclosure protected with thorns; ceping (Chipping Norton) a market place; ham (Balham) a village; geat (Margate) a gap in the cliffs; burgh, a place of fortification; the ingas and dens of Kent and Sussex (Hastings, Tenterden, Bidenden) and the hursts which meant that spaces had been cleared in the woods so that a vill(age) could be built (Wadhurst, Hawkhurst).

The vill was arranged so that it contained woodland and meadow, land for grazing (common land) and land for cultivation. The arable land was divided into two or three large fields which, in turn, were shared between all who lived on the vill. So that no person had better land than his neighbour each large field was sub-divided into strips. Thus each member of the community (thane, cottar and gebur) had some fertile land and some which grew little. Each year one of the fields was cultivated with oats, rye, wheat or barley whilst the other was left fallow (uncultivated) and allowed to recover from the previous year's sowing. The oats, rye and wheat were ground in the thane's water mill to give flour; the barley was used to make ale. Cattle, sheep and goats grazed on the common land and on the field left fallow, their dung providing fertilizer for next year's crop. The woodland provided pasture for pigs. We must remember, of course, that these animals were much smaller than those we see today. The cow, for example, was half the size of a Devon Red or Hereford, the full grown chicken no bigger than a bantam hen, whilst the Saxon pig grew to about two thirds the size of his modern descendent.

Beekeeping was also important. Honey was used both for sweetening food and to make mead, a strong alcoholic drink. A supply of salt had also to be maintained. This was used to preserve meat through the winter and was obtained by boiling sea water or from inland salt springs (as at Droitwich in Worcestershire).

The Anglo Saxons were also traders. In exchange for wool, cloth and slaves they obtained purple silk, jewels, gold, dyes, wine, oil, ivory latten (used by bell founders) brass, tin and glass. These goods came from far afield—bronze dishes from France, Egypt and Greece; shells and ivory from India; amethyst from North Africa; glass from Belgium. How can we be sure of this? We know, for example, that Anglo Saxon pottery was simple. It was hand cast. Some of the pottery which has been found in graves, however, was turned on a wheel and is identical to that made in Northern France. Again the early Anglo Saxon settlers in Britain did not make glass. No workshop sites have been found in Britain. Yet there are many examples in our museums of squat jars, pouch cups and claw beakers fashioned in glass, identical to those made in continental Europe.

The Anglo Saxons were also fine craftsmen, making brooches, pins and bracelets in gold and silver and engraving beautiful mounts for jewellery made of garnet and lapis lazuli. Their skill can also be seen in the beauty of their illuminated manuscripts.

Barter (the exchange of one sort of goods for another) is not an efficient way to carry on business. By the end of the sixth century, mints producing gold and silver coins had been established in London and Kent. Some time in the ninth century the value of the pound was fixed at 240 silver pennies with 12 silver pennies to the shilling. Much of the silver used for this coinage came from mines in Germany and was earned by the export of wool.

It is interesting to note that although the Viking people (Danes, Norwegians, Swedes) used silver for trading, they were more concerned with the weight of silver exchanged in any transaction than the face value of the coin. Merchants carried small scales to weigh silver. If the coins offered were too light, the weight was made up by adding further whole coins, or even by cutting coins into halves and quarters until the agreed weight of silver was achieved. Much silver entered Europe as a result of Viking trading with the Arabs and quantities of Arabian coins have been found in Viking settlements in north west Europe.

It is unlikely that the Danes (or Vikings) altered the normal pattern of farming. As we shall see, the open field system continued into Norman times. A Viking farm excavated in the Shetlands tells us a little about the animals which were kept, for the bones of oxen, sheep, pigs, dogs and ponies were found. These farmers did not only rely solely on food which they grew, however, for the remains of whale, numerous birds, deer and fish were also uncovered.

Most of the Danish tools (spades, hoes and forks) were made from wood. Wooden sledges and wooden two wheeled carts, both common in Scandinavia, travelled fairly easily over rough ground and with the sickle, scythe and plough probably made up the basic equipment of the farmer. If the account written in 1000 by Aelfric, Abbot of Eynsham, is accurate the plough was far from efficient. It required eight oxen to pull it and even then a plough boy had to continually prod the oxen with a goad to persuade them to move.

Much of the clothing worn by the common people (Anglo Saxon and Dane) was made entirely within the village. The wool from the village sheep was first cleaned and then spun on a hand spindle (distaff). After spinning the thread was woven into cloth on free standing wooden looms, the warp (the threads which run the length of the fabric) being kept taut with stones or weights made from clay.

The Norman system of farming was similar to that practised by the Anglo Saxons but with one big difference. All land was owned by the king. The king leased the land to his barons, who in turn leased it to lesser lords. These lesser lords leased the land to their villagers. Each person (be he a great lord or the poorest person in the poorest village) held his land in return for

Harold I
The head of Harold I, the last Anglo Saxon King of England, on a silver penny.
This photograph has been enlarged three times. (Photograph British Museum)

services he gave to his superior. Thus the barons held land from their king in return for their service at time of war, and the meanest villager (the villein) held land in return for working on his lord's estate. This service was defined by custom and it included a variety of work; labouring on the lord's land two days each week, ploughing for his lord in spring and autumn, reaping, fetching salt and fish and carting wood.

A small number of peasants (bordars) also had land holdings, but because they were much smaller than the villein's they had less duties to perform for the lord. Often they became village craftsmen, doing jobs for payment—usually in the form of corn.

Open fields—divided into strips—were cultivated on each Norman manor (the Anglo Saxon vill). Two fields were cultivated every year, wheat or rye being sown in the spring in one field, oats or barley in the autumn in another. The third remained fallow. Each strip was about 220 yards long by 22 yards wide. This was considered the amount which one man could plough in one day with one team of oxen. This gives us one acre ($220 \times 22 = 4840$ square yards). A hide—100 acres—was regarded as the amount of land a man would need to cultivate to support his family. As it was also the area which a team of eight oxen could be expected to plough in one year, we have some idea how hard it must have been to provide food for a family (100 acres equals $50\frac{1}{2}$ full-sized football pitches).

Not everybody, of course, was tied to the land in this way. There were quite large towns in Norman England in which merchants and traders and craftsmen in metal, wood and cloth earned their living. But dependence upon agriculture meant that farming and food production were of tremendous importance. The land was the source of power and this power was in the hands of the king.

Sheep's Head. South wall, Church of St Mary and St David, Kilpeck, Hereford and Worcester
Throughout Saxon and Norman times the sheep occupied a central part in the life of the farmer. Its carcass provided meat and its fleece wool for clothing. (Photograph Henry Pluckrose)

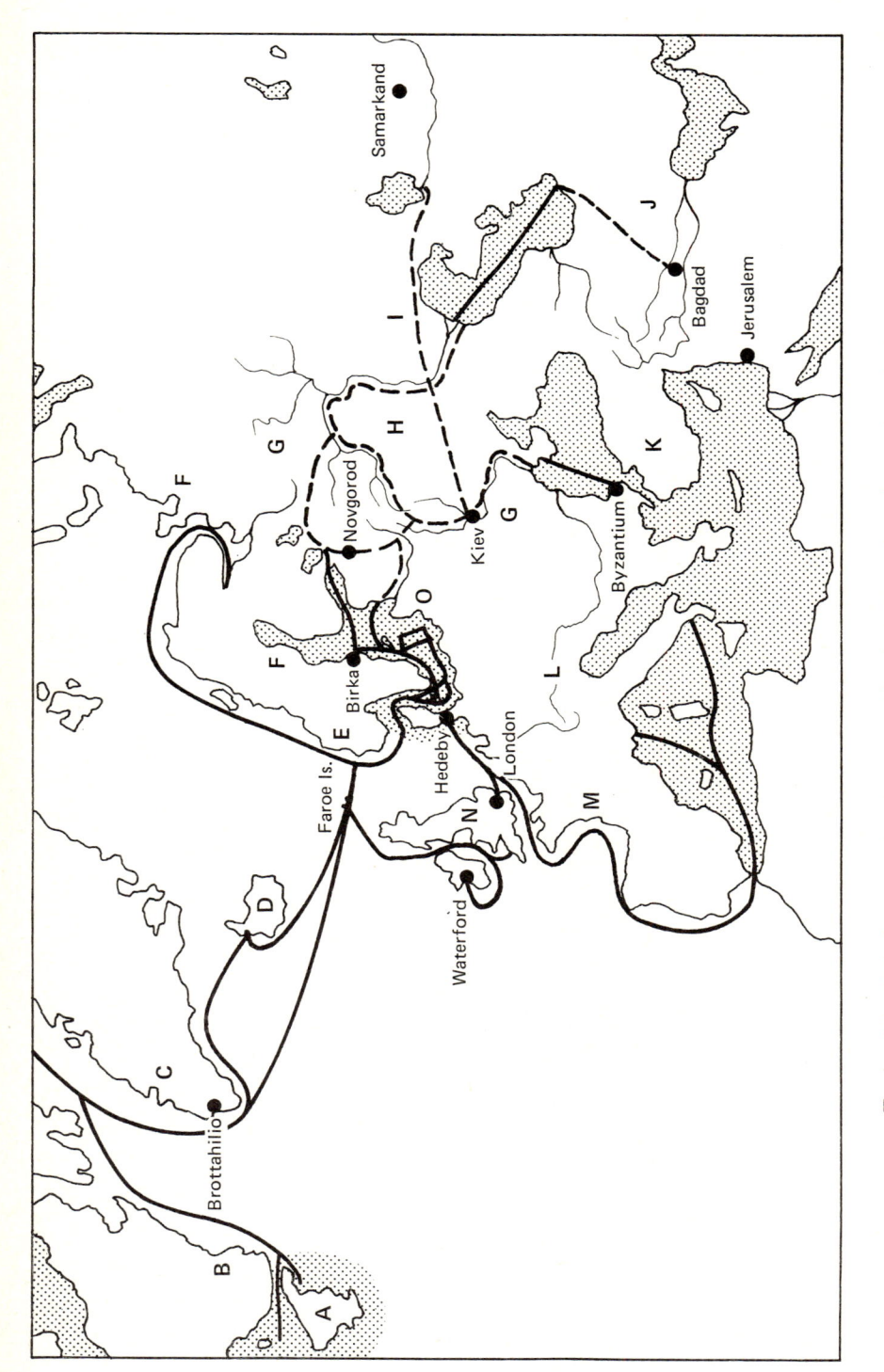

Trade—9th, 10th Century, showing sea and land routes and products of particular areas.

A Furs
B Timber
C Walrus, Ivory, Furs, Hides, Falcons, Woollens
D Fur, Fish, Woollens
E Timber
F Fur
G Slaves
H Slaves, Fur, Wax, Honey
I Silver
J Silk, Silver, Spices,
K Silk, Fruit, Spices, Wine, Jewellery
L Wines, Pottery, Glass, Cloth, Weapons, Jewellery
M Salt, Wine
N Wheat, Woollens, Tin, Honey
O Amber

4 at play

Sutton Hoo Lyre
This reconstruction of the Sutton Hoo Lyre can be seen in the British Museum. Its six strings (157.4 cm or 20¼ in. in length) were made from gut or horse hair, the bridge from bone, wood or amber, and the pegs from poplar or willow. Discoloration on the fragments of the lyre suggest that it was kept in a bag of beaver skin with the fur turned inwards.
(Photograph Henry Pluckrose)

Leisure (or time in which to follow our own hobbies and interests) would have seemed a strange idea to many of our ancestors. In Saxon, Viking and Norman times life was far from easy. Considerable effort had to be made to provide sufficient food to keep a family through the hard months of winter. Even if the harvest was good and the winter mild there was wood to cut and carry, wool and flax to spin, weave and dye and buildings to repair. However, it would be wrong to imagine that life was one long round of labour.

We know, for example, that the Saxons enjoyed playing a game very similar to our modern draughts, that they gambled on dice. We also know that they made music.

The New Forest, Nr Upper Canterton, Hampshire
King William I created the New Forest so that he had woodlands in which he could hunt. Some Anglo Saxon villages were destroyed in the process.

Severe penalties were imposed upon anyone who killed the royal deer.
(Photograph Janet & Colin Bord)

A six stringed lyre (a kind of harp) was found in the Sutton Hoo excavation. It was obviously a valuable instrument and treasured by the owner. Discoloration on the lyre suggests that it was kept in a bag made of beaver skin, with the fur turned inwards to give it greater protection.

Most Viking remains provide evidence of similar indoor pastimes. They played a number of games on chequered boards, including chess. These games did not always end peacefully. King Cnut quarrelled with his brother-in-law, Ulf, over a chess move in which Cnut lost his knight. A few days later Ulf was found murdered, probably by Ivar White, one of Cnut's bodyguards.

This story tells us something of another Viking pastime, that of story telling. The death of Earl Ulf was told so often by Viking minstrels that it passed into folk lore (or legend) which is how we come to know of the story today. The minstrels (called skalds) set the sagas (stories) to music, accompanying themselves on a lyre. These sagas also provide background to the things people believed and the way in which they lived. For example, they tell us that a Viking feast might include juggling, clowning, wrestling, dancing, gambling with dice and asking riddles. A crueller sport was horse fighting in which two horses would be tethered close together and provoked by their owners to kick and bite until one of the horses fell senseless.

Outdoor sports were probably similar to those of our own time. We know, again from the sagas, that running, rock throwing and boulder lifting were popular and that race meetings, regattas and swimming competitions were regularly held. One sport peculiar to the Vikings was oar walking. Here each competitor had to try to move the length of the ship, balancing above the water and jumping from one oar to the next. Meanwhile the oarsmen rowed with the intention of causing the 'walker' to fall into the sea.

No doubt some of these activities continued into Norman times. Certainly hunting (which was popular with the Vikings) was continued and extended by William and his followers. The Great Forests which covered Britain were declared 'royal'. This protected the deer and wild boar, which could only be hunted by the court, and meant that the forests in which they lived could not be cut back. The lesser nobility (abbots and barons) were allowed to hunt, but they could only catch and kill smaller animals like the hare and the fox.

The White Tower, London (*overleaf*)
The White Tower was one of two stone castles (or donjons) built during the reign of William the Conqueror. It was begun in the 1070s and is amongst the largest stone keeps in Western Europe. It was built under the direction of Bishop Gundulf in white stone quarried in Caen in Normandy. The Tower was one of three castles built to control London (the others, Baynards Castle and Montfichet have long since disappeared). These castles were far from popular with the Saxons. The Anglo Saxon Chronicler reporting William's death in 1087 observes 'He had castles built and poor men oppressed'.
(Photograph Kenneth Scowen)

5 at war

Having pushed the Britons into Wales and Cornwall, it was the turn of the Saxons to defend the land they had conquered. This they did by surrounding their towns (which were called burghs) with a ditch. Beyond the ditch was a steep embankment topped by a wooden palisade. This fence of interwoven stakes was kept in good repair throughout the year and given a thorough overhaul during May when labour could usually be spared from the farms.

Offa (757–796), King of Mercia and overlord of all the kingdoms south of the Humber, used a similar ditch and embankment construction to define the limits of this territory between the River Severn and the River Dee. 'Offa's Dyke' (as it came to be called) took in all the strategic ground over the 120 miles of its length. Unlike Hadrian's Wall, it was not built as a defensive barrier. Its purpose was to serve as a check upon tribesmen from the Welsh hills. If they did cross the dyke and were captured, they could hardly argue that they did not know they were trespassing in Mercia.

Grave finds (including such rich discoveries as that of Sutton Hoo) give a clear idea of the weapons which would have

Offas Dyke, near Edenhope Hill, Shropshire
Ethelbald, King of Mercia, had an earth wall erected along the western border of his territory. It was built by a person called 'Wat'.

Offa, who succeeded Ethelbald in 757, built a much more impressive wall which ran from the River Severn in the South to the River Dee in the North. This wall has come to be known as Offas Dyke. It consisted of a ditch on the western side (facing his likely enemies, the Welsh tribesmen) and a wall. The wall, which is 160 km (120 miles) long was 3 m high and 9 m broad.
(Photograph Picturepoint Ltd.)

Anglo Saxon pommel (Sutton Hoo)
The grip of the sword was made from horn or wood. The sword itself was made to the individual requirements of each warrior and great care was taken to achieve correct balance. Carrying a sword was a mark of rank, but the owner of this sword shown here was particularly important. On the pommel there is a ring—and these were only given as a sign of royal favour.
(Photograph Henry Pluckrose)

been carried by a Saxon warrior. Three of these; the axe, the spear and the knife were used in his everyday working life. The axe (the Francisca) had first been developed to clear woodland for farming, but being finely balanced it could be thrown with great accuracy. Similarly the spear, which was developed for hunting, could also be used in war. It could also be thrown at an enemy, but like the axe suffered from the disadvantage that it could always be picked up and thrown back! To prevent this happening a special throwing spear, the argon, was designed to bend on impact. Thus even if the argon only lodged in an enemy shield it made the shield much more awkward to handle in battle. The knife was worn by Saxon men and women as part of their everyday dress. The fighting knife, or Scramasax, was rather larger than the dress knife, but unlike a sword it had only one cutting edge.

In addition to these weapons the most important warriors also carried a sword, for a sword indicated rank and power. It was made with great care, the blade being specially welded to make it less brittle, its grip beautifully carved in horn or wood. Even the scabbard was lined with wool or fur to keep the blade free from dust.

Sutton Hoo Shield
The Sutton Hoo Shield (reconstructed using the original gilt bronze fitment) can be seen in the British Museum. It was made from three separate sheets of lime wood which were joined together and covered in calf hide. The edge was protected with leather. The iron boss in the centre gave protection to the warrior's hand. The diameter of the shield is 80 m (2½ ft).
(Photograph Henry Pluckrose)

Helmet, Sutton Hoo Ship Burial
This photograph illustrates the problem of constructing the past from objects found in graves. Firstly, the pieces of the Sutton Hoo Helmet had to be carefully cleaned. Then an attempt had to be made to reassemble them, which must have been rather like trying to complete a jigsaw with many pieces missing. (Photograph British Museum)

All of these were offensive weapons. To defend himself the thane would have worn a helmet and a shirt of mail (a war net or byrnie). His shield (like that found at Sutton Hoo) might have been fashioned from several sheets of lime wood, covered with calf hide and edged with leather.

The Dane armed for battle looked very similar to his Saxon counterpart. Again great attention was given to the sword, a two edged weapon of iron, strengthened with strands of steel wire and having a highly decorated hilt. Each sword was made to meet the individual requirements of a warrior and no two swords were alike. The long-handled battle axe with a triangular blade was also a popular weapon. It was often so heavy that it had to be held with two hands. The Danish foot soldier (or carl) also carried a spear.

For protection the warrior wore a tunic of leather strengthened with bone and an iron or leather helmet. He carried a shield. The face of the shield was strengthened with strips of metal, often representing the heads of snakes and birds. In its centre, a decorated boss protected the hand of the warrior. Each shield was made with a central hand hole and the metal boss was built over this.

The helmets of the jarls (chiefs) were more richly decorated than those of the carls, being faced with silver or bronze plate. The richer jarl might also have worn a corselet made from interlocking rings of iron.

The Danes also fought on horseback, their bowmen being able to fire from the saddle. This was only possible after the introduction (in about 920) of the 'T' and 'H' shaped bridle bit, a design they copied from the Magyar horsemen of Hungary.

Although the Danes did not bring horses with them on their cross channel raids, the long ships were designed so that animals could be carried. The ships had a very shallow draft. If horses and cattle were being unloaded they were encouraged to move on to the side of the ship nearest the land. This caused it to tip making the jump from ship to shore easy for the animals to manage.

The long boat was really a war machine, for it enabled the Danish warriors to move close to the shore and along shallow rivers and waterways. No complete Danish ship has been found in Britain, but an idea of their size can be gained from the Gokstad ship which can be seen in Oslo. Made from overlapping planks of oak, this ship was 23.2 m long, 5.25 m wide and a maximum of 1.95 m deep at midships. It carried a squat rectangular sail made of wool and strengthened with strips of leather. There were places of 32 oars, the shields of the rowers being lashed in special holes along its sides. At sea the warriors lived on cold food, but the cauldrons which were also found aboard could hold as much as 32 gallons (145 litres), big enough to heat soup or porridge for 50 men.

The army which fought against William of Normandy at Hastings would have been equipped similarly to the Danes described above. The weapons of the Normans, however, were rather more sophisticated. The knight wore a coat of mail (slit back and front to make riding more comfortable) over a linen tunic. His head was protected by a round helmet which had a nose piece attached and his thighs by leg armour, called greaves. He carried a kite shaped shield. His principal weapons were the sword and the mace.

The Norman knights on the Bayeux tapestry are shown using stirrups, which means that they could also use a lance without the danger of them being unseated on impact with an enemy. The knights were supported by archers who fired from a short bow.

William's victory at Hastings would have been of little value had he not also been able to control the country afterwards. To this end he built fortified donjons (safe places or keeps) in strategic positions.

enclosure and a moat. Only two stone castles were built during William's reign (1066–1087) and these were at London and Colchester. However, the wooden castles were effective. The Domesday survey showed that in 1086 there were 5,000 knights to man 250 castles, a garrison of about 20 knights per castle.

The development of armed knight and fortified castle caused a new pattern of warfare to develop, a pattern which was to last until castle walls could be easily breached and armour no longer gave adequate protection to the knight.

This new weapon—and it does not concern us here—was gunpowder.

Statue of Harold, Waltham Abbey, Essex
This statue of Harold holding the Abbey he built in his left hand is comparatively modern. Statues such as this often include inaccuracies in such things as dress and armour and are not, therefore, a very reliable source of historical material.
(Photograph Henry Pluckrose)

These donjons—we now call them castles—were places to which his soldiers could retreat if faced by superior forces. They were also centres from which the countryside could be administered and controlled.

The first castles built by the Normans were of wood. The keep was usually erected on a rise in the land surrounded by an

Castle Rising, Norfolk *(overleaf)*
It is not certain when the earthworks at Castle Rising were first thrown up. They may date from Roman times. This photograph illustrates how a keep was given additional protection by being enclosed by an earth rampart (19 m high) and a moat. At Castle Rising the keep was also protected by two smaller enclosures to the East and to the West.
(Photograph Aerofilms Ltd.)

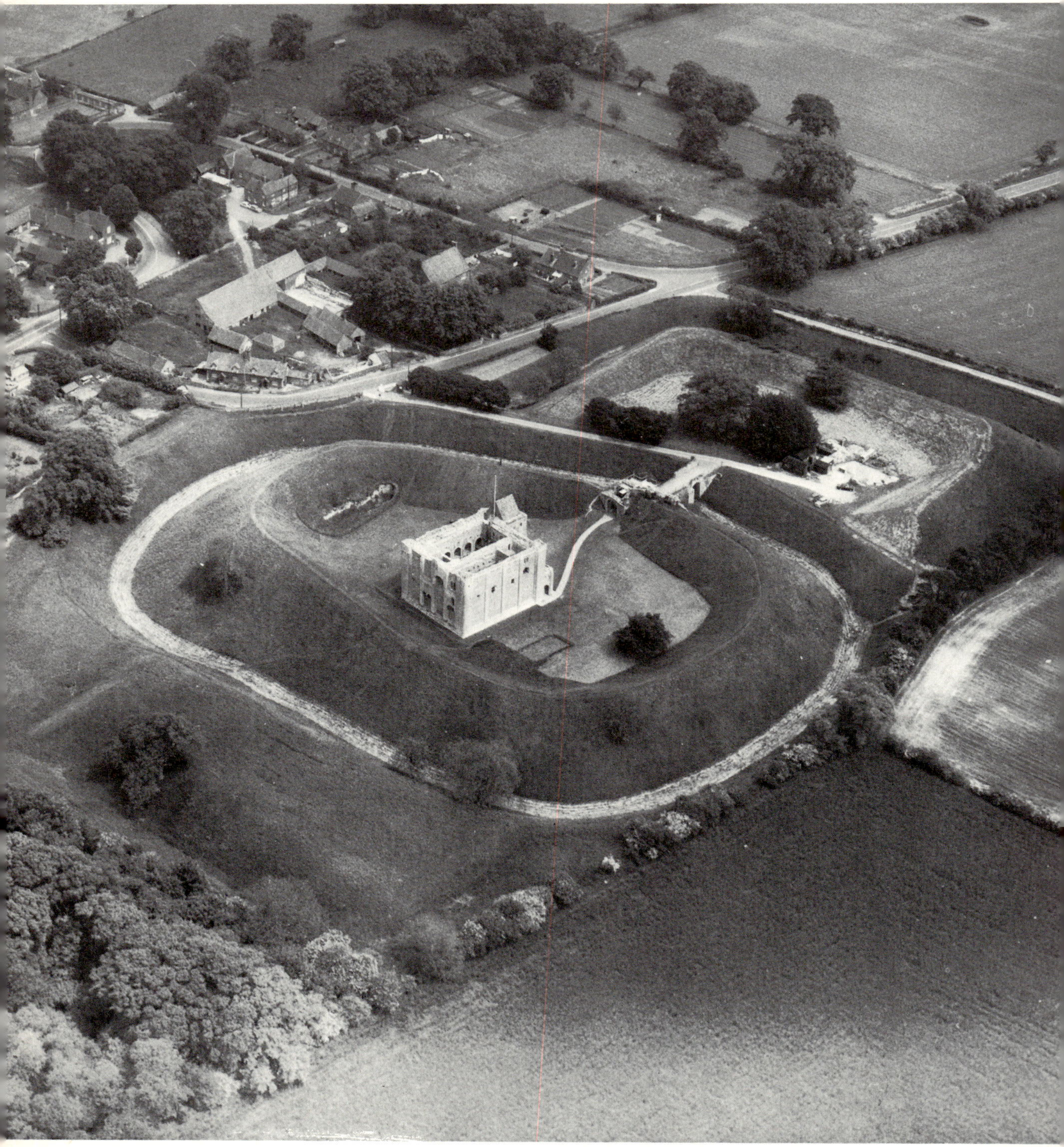

Colchester Castle, Essex
Colchester Castle, one of the two stone castles built in the lifetime of William I, was erected on the site of a former Roman temple. Many fragments of Roman brick and tile are incorporated in its walls.
(Photograph A. F. Kersting)

Pleshey Castle, Nr Chelmsford, Essex
Pleshey Castle is a motte and bailey castle. The motte (or mound) which is the top photograph on which the castle stood is surrounded by a moat. Around the motte is the bailey, a flat enclosure encircled by earthen walls beyond which lies another moat. In Norman times a wooden bridge joined the bailey to the motte.
Pleshey Castle was built by Geoffrey de Mandeville, Sherriff of Essex and Hertfordshire and High Constable of England on land held by him from William the Conqueror.
(Photographs Henry Pluckrose)

6
At Law

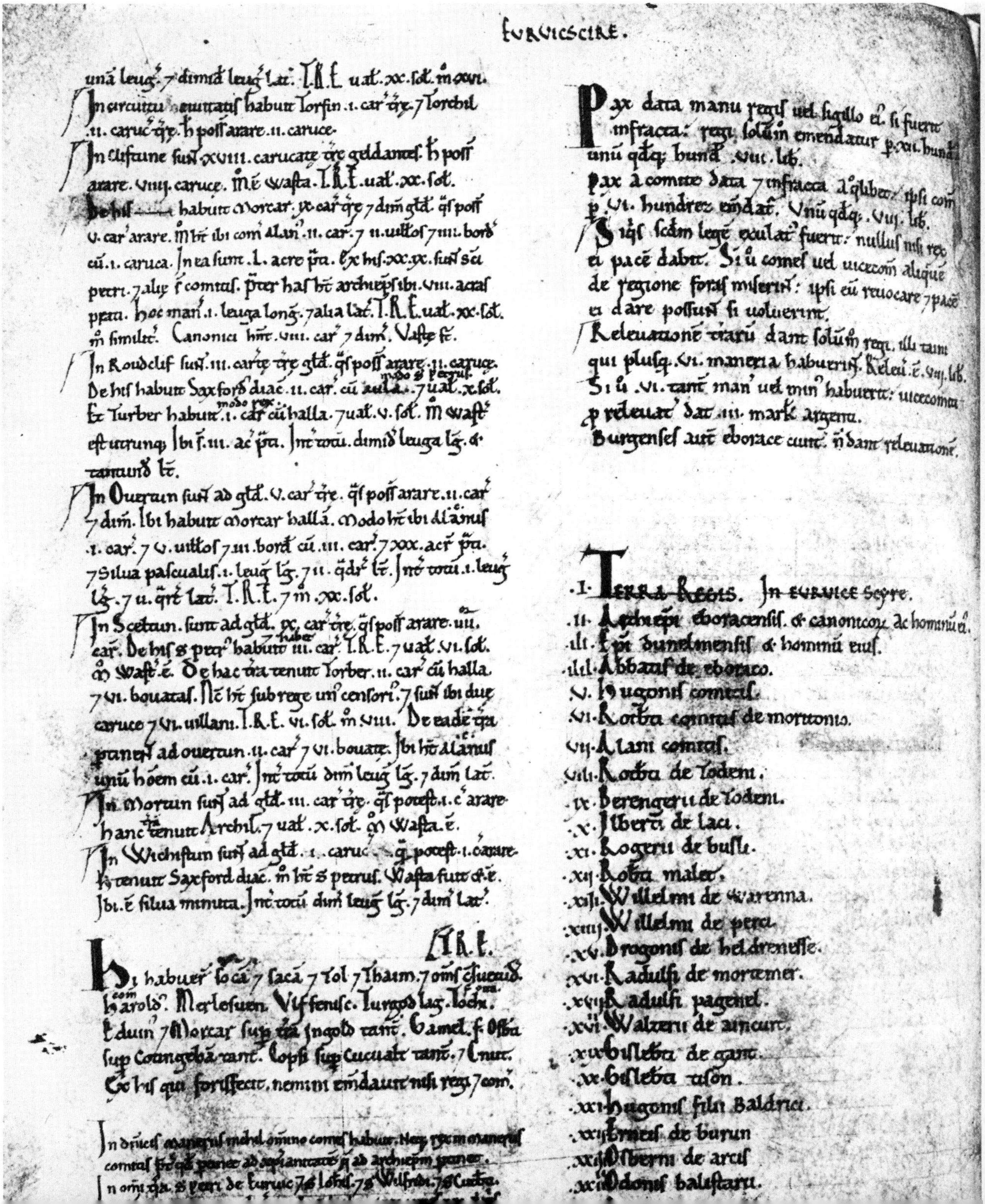

EVRVICSCIRE.
.I. TERRA REGIS. In Euruicscyre.
.II. Archiepi eboracensis & canonicor. & hominu ei.
.III. Epi dunelmensis & hominu eius.
.IIII. Abbatis de eboraco.
.V. Hugonis comitis.
.VI. Rotbti comitis de moritonio.
.VII. Alani comitis.
.VIII. Rotbti de todeni.
.IX. Berengerii de todeni.
.X. Ilberti de laci.
.XI. Rogerii de busli.
.XII. Robti malet.
.XIII. Willelmi de warenna.
.XIIII. Willelmi de perci.
.XV. Drogonis de heldrenesse.
.XVI. Radulfi de mortemer.
.XVII. Radulfi pagenel.
.XVIII. Walterii de aincurt.
.XIX. Gisleberti de gant.
.XX. Gisleberti tison.
.XXI. Hugonis filii Baldrici.
.XXII. Ernegis de burun.
.XXIII. Osberni de arcis.
.XXIIII. Odonis balistarii.

The Domesday Book (*previous page*)
The Domesday survey was really a giant reference book, originally known as the 'Book of the Treasury'. The king's clerks sorted out the answers given to the investigators and wrote them down county by county in two volumes. The careful organization of their findings meant that the king could see exactly how much land each tenant-in-chief held.
(Photograph Public Record Office)

The first chapter explained how the Anglo Saxons settled in Britain and formed a number of small separate kingdoms. Each of these kingdoms had its own king and its own laws. The rise of Wessex in the ninth century and the defeat of Guthrum by Alfred helped unite the country but it was not until the reign of King Canute (1016–1035) that Saxon and Dane could be considered as one people.

The Anglo Saxon king (and the Danish kings who ruled England after Ethelred) ruled through the Witan, a council of wise men.

The Saxon idea of government was that all men were free. They could own land and claim protection of the king's law. In exchange for these rights each man paid tax and could be asked to carry arms. Thus the king was an overlord who, supported by his earls, thegns and housecarls (the noble families), ruled over a population of churls (or free peasants). In return for his overlordship the king enjoyed certain profitable rights on the land and was allowed to impose gelds (or taxes) on his subjects.

The country was divided into shires and each shire into hundreds. In each shire the king's reeve (or sheriff) saw that the king's rights were maintained. In the shire court

King Alfred: Statue in the Town Centre, Wantage, Berkshire
Wantage was one of the old towns of Wessex. This statue of Alfred, who was born in Wantage in 849, was designed by Count Gleichen. It was erected in 1877. He is shown wearing the dress of a Saxon earl and holding a large battle axe. Note the triangular shaped blade.
(Photograph A. F. Kersting)

the king's rulings and wishes were made known in the form of writs to his ealdormen and thegns. Each hundred also had a court which met monthly. At this court wrongdoers were punished and the king's laws imposed. Within each hundred, freemen, in groups of ten men known as tithings, were also given responsibility (rather like monitors and prefects in school) for the good behaviour of their area or village.

King William always claimed that he wanted to preserve the laws of Edward the Confessor. However, his reign marks an important change in the way the country was governed.

The Norman king was the lord of all the land. He granted land to his most important barons and the bishops, in exchange for knight service. These 'tenants in chief' (so called because they held their land from the king) then re-let part of their lands to a lesser baron who, in turn, might re-let an even smaller part to an even less important baron. The lands of the tenants in chief were spread across the country so that no one baron could become powerful by holding too much land in any one area. By leasing as 'fiefs', land in this way, the church and the barons were expected to provide the king with the services of 6,000 armed knights for a total of 40 days a year.

This exchange of duties for land (known as feudalism) continued right down to village level. The lord of the manor held all the land. He leased this to his peasants (villeins or cottars) in exchange for their labour. He would also give them the protection of his own court, but they were not free. They were tied to the village for life.

William's hold on England was tightened by the Domesday survey. This was begun in 1085 when teams of inquisitors were sent to every part of the country. At special courts they recorded returns from barons, shire reeves, priests and peasants and noted who held each piece of land, the size of each holding, the number of villagers, the animals and ploughs they owned, the character of the estate (woodland, grazing, marsh) and its value. So thorough was the survey that 'not even one ox, or one cow, or pig escaped notice'.

To really appreciate the degree of detail in the survey, it is best to look at the insertion for a particular village. For example, Kilpeck in Herefordshire is recorded as follows.

'These towns or lands underwritten are

William I
The head of William I on a Norman silver penny. This photograph has been enlarged three times. (Photograph British Museum)

Edward the Confessor
An Anglo-Saxon silver penny showing the head of Edward the Confessor. Edp (=w)ard Rex.
This photograph has been enlarged three times. (Photograph British Museum)

situated on the border of Archenfeld. William Fitz Norman holds Chipecce (Kilpeck). Cadcard held it in the time of King Edward. In the demesne (lord's land) are three plough hands and two bondsmen and four ploughmen and 57 men with ploughlands and they pay 15 quails of honey and ten shillings. They do not give other tribute nor do service except in the army. Value, four pounds.'

We could say that Norman feudalism did not give ordinary men as much freedom as they had had under the Saxon and Danish kings. But this is to suggest that before William came the peasant was able to move as he pleased or to change his way of life.

The Normans did not turn Saxon freemen into slaves. They noted the customs of the people and made these customs the basis of their laws.

The church of St. Mary & St. David, Kilpeck, Herefordshire
Kilpeck was given to William Fitz Norman by William I. The church, which was begun after 1100, was built on the same site as a Saxon church and incorporates some of this earlier building into its walls. Modern Kilpeck remains a small community, hardly larger than the 66 menfolk recorded in the Domesday survey. (Photograph Henry Pluckrose)

Westminster Hall, London
Westminster Hall was built by William Rufus in 1097 and formed part of the mediaeval Old Palace of Westminster. The hall as we see it today, however, dates from 1394, when it was re-designed for King Richard II. The hall has been used for many famous trials, like those of Sir Thomas More (1535) and Charles I (1649). More recently it has been used for occasions of state ceremonial.
(Photograph A. F. Kersting)

The coast at Dunwich, Suffolk
The village of Dunwich is also mentioned in the Domesday book. In mediaeval times the sea slowly eroded the coast and many of its houses, churches and monasteries were washed away. Today little of Dunwich remains. The Domesday survey (and similar old documents) help historians to understand and to plot the changing face of our landscape.
(Photograph A. F. Kersting)

7 at prayer

We know that Christianity survived in the British Isles after the Romans had departed. The Celtic Church, as we saw in Chapter 1, was kept alive in Scotland and Ireland. From this base missionaries began to bring the Gospel to the people living in the north at about the same time as the monks, led by St. Augustine, were converting the people of Kent.

The Saxons were a pagan people. They brought to Britain their own Gods of whom Woden, Tiw, Thunor, Frig and Eostre were the most important. Since religion is concerned with both life on earth and the life which is to come after death, we learn a great deal about the things people believed by studying their burial practices.

The Saxons seemed to have used two methods of disposing of the dead. In early Saxon times cremation was general, the body being burned and the ashes placed in a pot (or urn) and buried. These pot burials were very simple and very few objects were placed beside the pot in the grave.

The second method of burial was much more complicated. The body was buried with all the goods he might need for his journey into the next world. Men were buried with their weapons, women with their jewellery. At Petersfinger, near Salisbury, for example, the body of a Saxon soldier was excavated in 1948. His grave contained fragments of linen and wool and evidence of a shield, a spear, a knife, a belt and buckle and a drinking pot. Sometimes, if the dead person was of considerable importance he might be buried in a ship, which was lowered into the ground and covered by a great mound of earth.

The Sutton Hoo treasure was found in a 'ship barrow' of this sort. It was probably the funeral monument to King Raedwald of East Anglia who died in about 624 A.D. King Raedwald was converted to Christianity, but before he died he probably returned to his earlier pagan beliefs. His tomb, a ship 27.4 m long contained a wealth of grave goods; silver from the Mediterranean, armour, ornate weapons, spoons and bowls. Now the interesting thing about this burial is that some of the goods were undoubtedly Christian. There was a bowl from Egypt engraved with a camel, a donkey and a lion, silver spoons marked with the names of Saulos and Paulos (Saul and Paul, a present to a royal convert to Christianity) and bowls decorated with the Cross. It is as though the people who buried King Raedwald wished to ensure an after life for their lord by incorporating both Christian and pagan practice in one grave.

This confusion continued even after Christianity had a firm hold. Many Christian graves have been uncovered which also contain a single pot. Was this an offering to God, an aid to the soul on its journey or simply the memory of a time when a pot contained the ashes of the dead? It was not until the eighth century that the Church was strong enough to enforce Christian burial, that the corpse was laid so that the feet pointed towards the east and the Holy Land.

The Vikings were also a pagan people. Their chief god was Odin who, they believed, was responsible for giving them the Runic alphabet. The runes were angular letters, particularly suitable for carving with a knife or chisel onto wood or stone. There were two runic alphabets each of 16 symbols of futharks (this word is made up from the sound made by the first letters of the most widely used Runic symbols— F U T H O R C). The runes were regarded as

St. Peters ad Vincula, Tower of London
The White Tower was completed in 1097 to the design of Gundulf, a Benedictine monk who became the Bishop of Rochester.

The tower was many things. It was a fortress, a prison, a palace and a place where royal treasures could be stored in safety. Because so many people lived and worked in the Tower, it is not surprising to learn that it had its own chapel. The style of building— heavy columns supporting round arches—is typically Norman.
(Photograph A. F. Kersting)

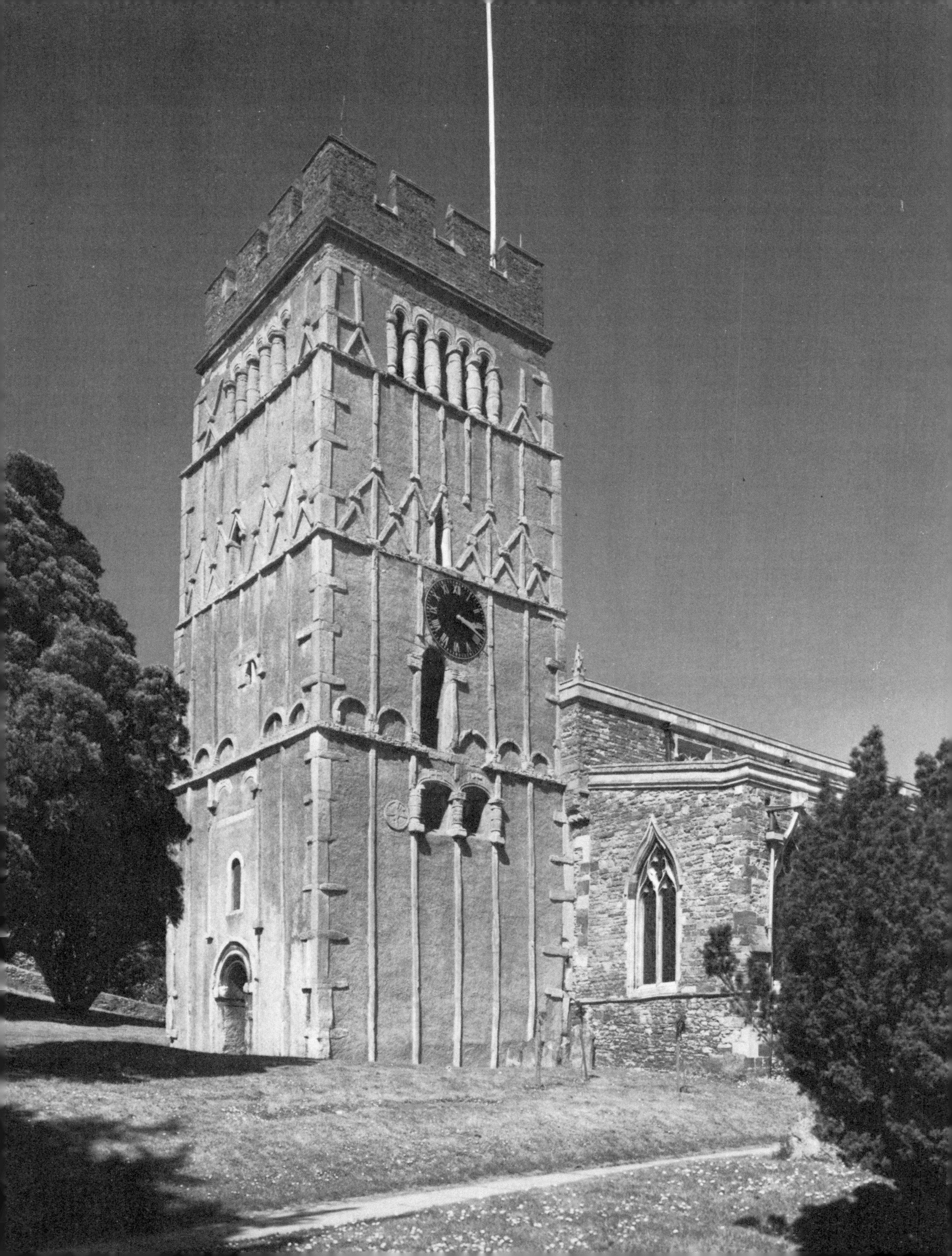

giving magic power and protection. In the Isle of Man, for example, there are 30 runic crosses. One reads 'Tola had this stone set up in memory of her son. In the east they gave the eagle food'. One other strange aspect of these inscriptions is that some were intended to be read from right to left and from the bottom of the stone to the top.

Runic Alphabet in its earliest form. Modern equivalents are as follows

f	u	th	a	r	k
g	w	h	n	i	y
p	e	r	s	t	b
e	m	l	ng	d	o

The church of All Saints, Earls Barton, Northamptonshire

The tower of this church is unusual. It was built between 900–1000 and was originally used as a place of refuge. Notice how the stones at the corners of the tower are arranged. This is called 'long and short work' and provides a useful means of identifying Saxon building. The reason for the pattern of triangles has never been satisfactorily explained. It has been suggested that the builder was attempting to copy in stone the patterns which would have appeared had he worked in wood.

The Saxon tower ends just below the brick battlements which were added in the 15th century. (Photograph A. F. Kersting)

Viking burials were as varied as those of the Saxons. The Viking soldier would expect to be buried with all his weapons and his horse; the Viking smith and the Viking carpenter with his tools; the Viking lady with her jewels and her chatelaine (see page 38). If weapons were buried with the dead these were sometimes 'killed' too, the sword was bent double to prevent it being of any use to a grave robber. Ship burials were also practised by the Vikings. Sometimes this took the form of burial of the ship, sometimes the ship was surrounded with wood and set alight.

Even when the Vikings (Danes) were converted to Christianity after making peace with Alfred, they still tended to mix pagan belief with Christian practice. On the Theowald Cross at Andreas in the Isle of Man the Viking god Odin is being eaten by the wolf Ferris. On the other side of the slab is a figure bearing a cross and a bible.

Many Danes adopted Christ as an equal to their own Gods. In one saga the hero tells how he worships Christ on land, but Thor at sea. This mixture of faiths was also noted at Wensley in Yorkshire where a Christian graveyard was used for pagan style burial.

When trading, Danes who were not converted experienced some difficulty in dealing with Christian traders. This was easily overcome, however, by primsigning, a simple ceremony which involved making the sign of the cross on the doubting convert. As no water was used both Dane and Christian could ignore the 'baptism' if they wished to do so!

But, if the first raiders from Scandinavia killed many monks and burned many churches and holy places, when they were finally converted they became keen christians. The early missionaries to the Anglo Saxons had built small churches, often on pagan sites. Cathedrals and monasteries followed which, if small by the standards of the later Middle Ages, were places where the Christian message could be taught, learning fostered and men and women trained as priests, monks and nuns.

Saxon churches were built of wood, but for some, stone, tile and brick were used. Of these, a few remain. The Anglo Saxons found it difficult to span large spaces in stone and their buildings are, therefore, small and intimate. With the coming of the Normans a new style of building developed, a style which was to flower in the magnificent buildings of the medieval church.

St. Andrew's Church, Greensted Juxta Ongar, Essex

It is thought that pre Christian Celts tended to worship their Gods in the 'groves' (or woods). This area of Essex was once heavily forested and the church of St. Andrew might well have been built on an old pagan shrine. The wooden beams which form the nave of the church have been renewed down the centuries although some date from about the year 650. The church was enlarged and altered by the late Saxons (870), the Normans (1099) and the Tudors (1500). A large restoration programme was also undertaken in Victorian times, leaving the church much as we see it today. (Photograph A. F. Kersting)

The church of St. John the Evangelist, Escomb, County Durham
This little church has been described as the most perfect Saxon building in Britain. This is because the stones have been so carefully prepared and fashioned. It might be, of course, that the reason for this is that the stones were not prepared by Saxon builders, but simply taken from a nearby Roman ruin and re-used.
(Photograph A. F. Kersting)

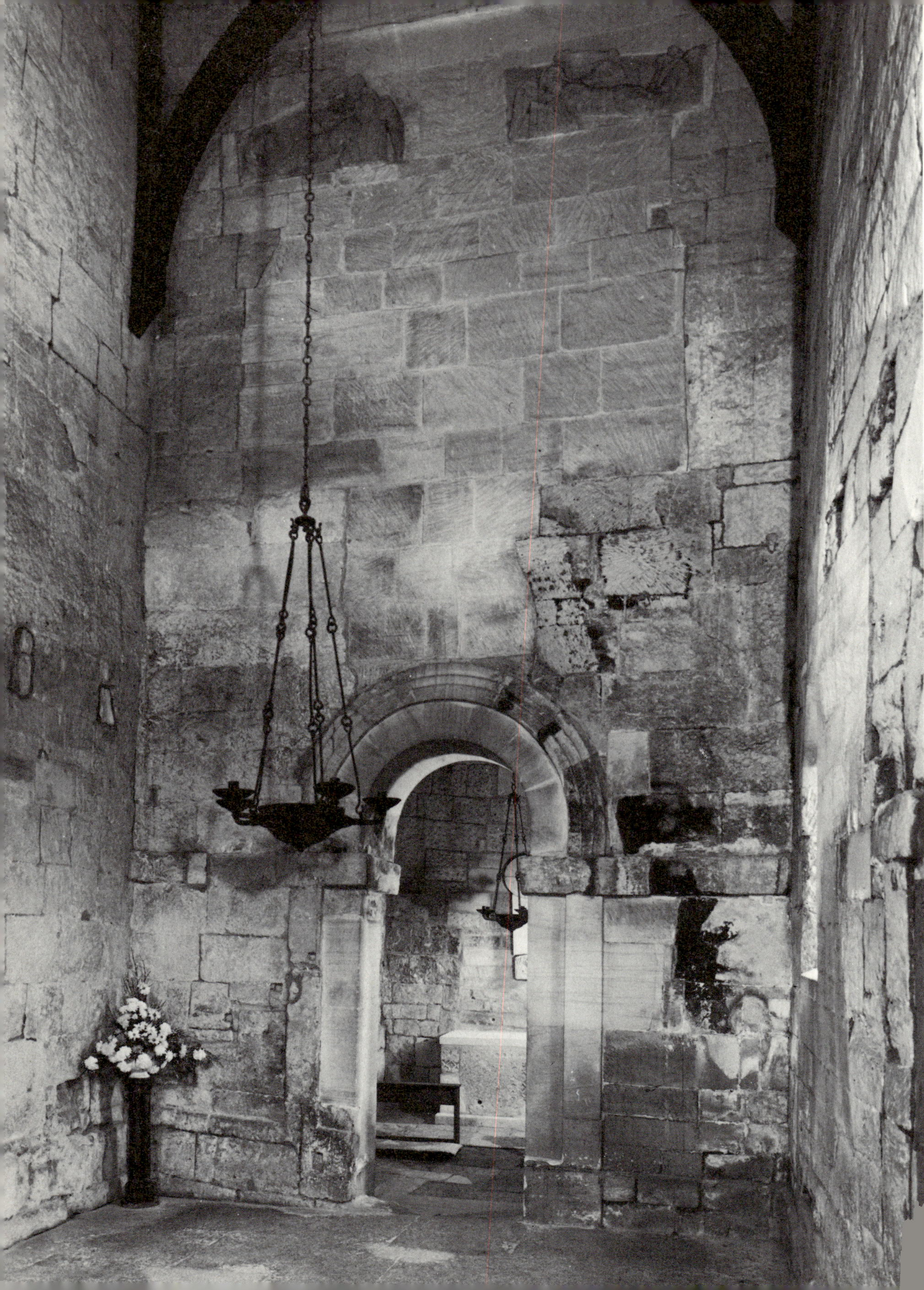

Church of St. Lawrence, Bradford-on-Avon, Wiltshire *(left)*
No one knows who built the church of St. Lawrence. It may have been one of the churches founded by St. Aldhelm, the Saint of Wessex, who lived in the 7th century. Aldhelm has been described as the singing saint. He set the bible stories to lively music and was prepared to break into song at the least excuse, even in a market place or by a river crossing.
(Photograph A. F. Kersting)

St. Cuthbert's stole, Durham Cathedral, County Durham
When St. Cuthbert died, in 687, his body was buried on Lindisfarne. When the Danes repeated their attacks on the monastery the monks fled. As St. Cuthbert had asked the community not to leave his body behind should they ever leave Lindisfarne, the monks took the shrine containing his bones with them. After years of wandering, the community settled at Durham. Here they founded a new monastery which was eventually to become Durham Cathedral.

Prayers at the shrine of the Saint were often supported by gifts of goods and money. Athelstan, King of the Anglo Saxons, presented a set of church vestments to the monks in 924. This is a stole, or priestly scarf.
(Photograph A. F. Kersting)

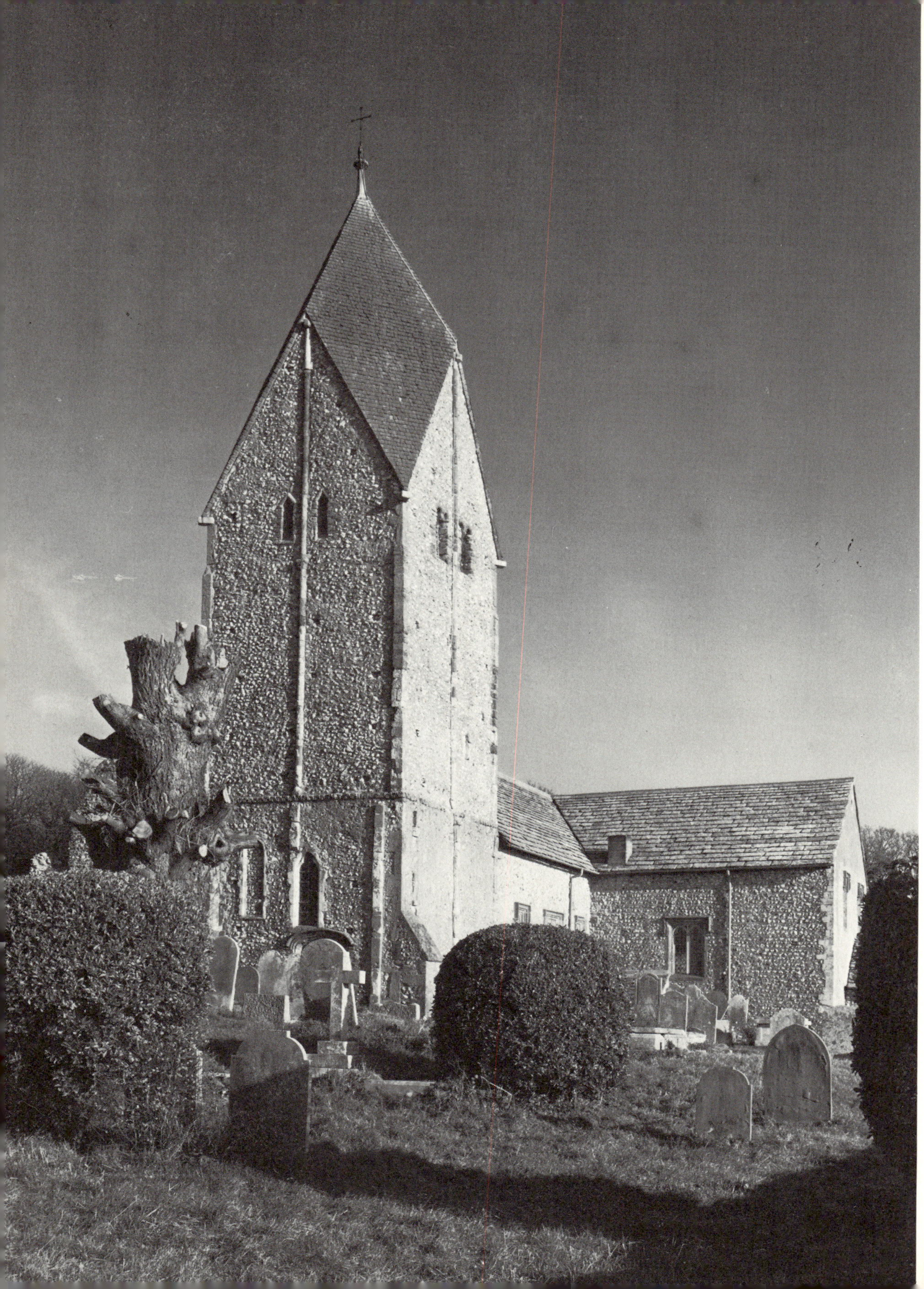

Church of St. Mary The Virgin, Sompting, Sussex
Sompting church is the only church in the British Isles with a four gabled spire (a 'Rhenish helm'). The tower dates from the Saxon period, but much of the church was rebuilt by the Knights Templars in the 12th century.
(Photograph A. F. Kersting)

All Saints Church, Brixworth, Northamptonshire
All Saints Church was founded in about 675 by monks who originally came from Lindisfarne, as a centre for Celtic missionaries to preach the gospel in the Kingdom of Mercia. The puzzling thing about this church is that although it was served by Celtic monks it looks very much like the early Italian churches. We do know, however, that the Bishop at this time, Wilfred of Hexham, often travelled in France and Italy. Perhaps he brought back craftsmen to help build the churches he was founding in England.
(Photograph Henry Pluckrose)

The tomb of Edward the Confessor, Westminster Abbey, London
As a young boy Edward spent much of his time in Normandy. When he returned to England he brought with him many Norman advisers. The abbey church which he built west of the city of London was sufficiently completed for him to be buried near the altar. In medieval times his tomb became a place of pilgrimage, for Edward's generosity towards the church had been considered particularly holy during his lifetime. When he died in 1066 he became the last saint of the old Anglo Saxon ruling house.
(Photograph A. F. Kersting)

Norman doorway and arches, Abbey church of the Holy Cross and St Lawrence, Waltham Abbey, Essex
The ruins of Richards Castle in Shropshire indicate that Norman ideas and techniques were influencing the English even before the invasion of 1066. The doorway and the arcading shown here are part of the church which Harold Godwinson founded in 1060.
(Photograph Henry Pluckrose)

William of Normandy's conquest of England

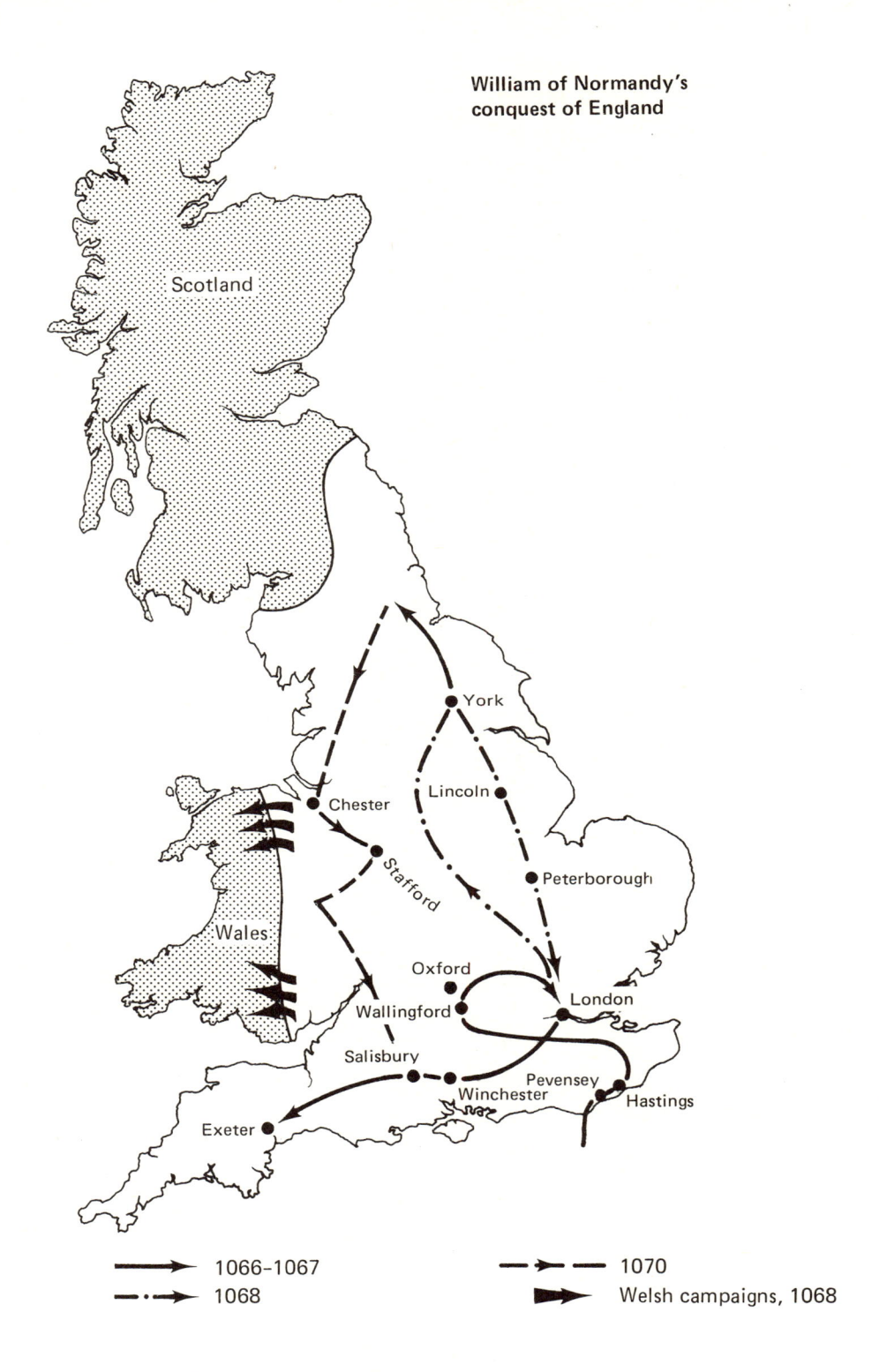

- → 1066–1067
- –·–▸ 1068
- ––▸ 1070
- ▶ Welsh campaigns, 1068

Norman doorway. The church of St Mary and St David, Kilpeck, Hereford and Worcester
The decorative style followed by early Norman masons is very similar to that of the Viking peoples of Scandinavia from whom they were descended. Certainly the twisted and whirled interlacings and the grotesque faces on the carvings over the south door of Kilpeck parish church seem to owe more to pagan tradition than to Christian practice.
(Photograph Henry Pluckrose)

museums of special interest

ANGLO SAXON ENGLAND (other than those specifically mentioned in the text)

Abingdon, Oxfordshire Town Museum
Arbroath, Angus St. Vigeans Museum
Battle, East Sussex Battle Museum
Cambridge University Museum of Archaeology
Canterbury, Kent St. Martin's Church
Colchester, Essex The Castle
Conway, Gweynedd Aberconway House
Durham, County Durham The Cathedral Undercroft
Ediburgh, Scotland National Museum of Antiquities
Evesham, Hereford & Worcester The Almonry Museum
Glastonbury, Somerset The Tribunal
Grantham, Lincolnshire The Museum
Grays, Essex Thurrock Local History Museum
Leicester, Leicestershire Jewry Wall Museum
Lewes, Sussex Barbican House Museum
Lindisfarne, Northumberland The Priory
Liverpool, Merseyside The County Museum
London and Greater London British Museum, W.C.1., Kingston-upon-Thames Museum, Museum of London, E.C.I
Meigle, Perth Meigle Museum
Newcastle-upon-Tyne, Northumberland Museum of Antiquities
Oakham, Leicestershire Rutland County Museum
Repton, Derbyshire Church of St. Wystan
Rothbury, Northumberland Ladyswell, nr Holystone
St. Andrews, Fife St. Andrew's Cathedral Museum
Shaftesbury, Dorset Abbey Ruins Museum
Whithorn, Wigtown Whithorn Priory Museum
Winchester, Hampshire Winchester Cathedral Library
York, Yorkshire Viking York Exhibition (York Archaeological Trust)